BUILDING EFFECTIVE LAY LEADERSHIP TEAMS

GEORGE BARNA

ISSACHAR RESOURCES
A DIVISION OF BARNA RESEARCH GROUP, LTD.
VENTURA, CALIFORNIA

Published by Issachar Resources, a division of the Barna
Research Group, Ltd., 5528 Everglades Street, Ventura, CA 93003.
All rights reserved. No portion of this book may be reproduced,
stored in a retrieval system or transmitted in any form or by any
means - electronic, mechanical, photocopy, computer scan,
recording or any other - except for brief quotations in printed reviews,
without the prior written permission of the publisher or author.

All Scripture quotations in this book, except where noted otherwise,
are from the Holy Bible: New International Version.
Copyright © 1973, 1978, 1984 by International Bible Society. Used
by permission of Zondervan Publishing House. All Rights Reserved.

Library of Congress Cataloging-in-Publication Data
Barna, George
Building Effective Lay Leadership Teams / George Barna
00-1088714
ISBN 0-9671372-2-5 Hardcover

Printed in Canada

TABLE OF CONTENTS

ACKNOWLEDGMENTS

Most of the books I have written have been a joy to produce, with ideas flooding my mind and words exploding onto the page, the result making sense even in the earliest drafts. This book has been the exception to that history. In spite of my passion to see godly leadership within the Church, and my zealous belief in the notion of team leadership, my writing schedule and frustrations put several people through unfortunate torture. I'd like to ask for their forgiveness, thank them for their patience, and applaud their perseverance.

The person who suffered the most has been my wife. Nancy held on as best she could, trying to carve out more and more time for me to sequester myself into hotel rooms and other available places, playing both mother and father to the girls during my labored writing days. This was especially difficult while we were traveling during our seminar tour, as I struggled to capture the proper focus and energy to write in-between travel days and speaking engagements. She is an incredible woman and a tremendous helper. My gratitude is also extended to my daughters, Samantha and Corban, who came in a close second in the abandonment contest. My buddies again forfeited daddy several days too many and, at times, when it was just plain unfair to do so. They rebounded with characteristic sympathy and enthusiasm. Thank you, girls, for loving me, praying for me and for this book every night, and for believing that we will schedule my time better in the future. You deserve nothing less.

I failed to spare my colleagues at Barna Research. Rachel Ables good-naturedly put up with delay after delay in the delivery of the manuscript, and held our editor, printers and customers at bay while I dawdled. Yes, the tardy and tortured delivery of this book is a good argument for gun control. Thanks, Rachel, for being a great sport about this and for cheerfully producing a tangible product, in spite of it all.

The rest of the team at Barna Research endured their suffering with smiling silence. (At last, a benefit of being "the boss.") Thank you, David Kinnaman, for keeping the show rolling along, despite my physical absence, my absent-mindedness when I was physically present, and my abject refusal to pay attention to project deadlines regardless of the nature of my absenteeism. Thank you, Meg Wells, Pam Jacob, and Carmen Moore, for flexing with project schedules while my laptop and I lost touch with reality. Thank you, Brooke McGrath, Jill Kinnaman, Irene Robles, and Celeste Rivera, for sticking to the plan even though I seemed to remain oblivious to it. Thank you, Julie Carobini, for unexpectedly becoming an "on call" editor, and to Kim Wilson of The Barna Institute, our "sister" non-profit organization that strives to support churches, for staying the course while I vanished.

My solace is knowing that God knows that "of making books there is no end" and therefore He is not disillusioned by my tardiness; that to the Lord, "a day is as a thousand years," further supporting my argument that being a few weeks late with a manuscript does not perturb the Lord; and that He loves me in spite of what I do, not because of it. I pray that the Lord will be able to use this book to inspire, instruct and improve thousands of ministries across the nation.

CHAPTER ONE

LEADERSHIP IS
MOST EFFECTIVE WHEN IT
COMES FROM TEAMS

I spend my days analyzing the state of our society in order to anticipate what is coming and inform church leaders of how those changes will affect our lives. Change, of course, is the defining attribute of our culture. Understanding the nature and direction of change can help people to maximize their abilities, enjoy life, and accomplish personal goals more consistently and efficiently.

For people to get the most out of life, however, they need to pursue a purposeful direction that provides meaning and significance to their existence. Our lives are comprised of a half dozen or so important dimensions that we intentionally and regularly nurture. Among the most common priorities are spirituality, family, career, community involvement, leisure, health, and intellectual development. We gain a sense of satisfaction and fulfillment from growing in these areas.

But how do we know what constitutes an appropriate direction to pursue? Sometimes we determine our direction by watching what others do and by mimicking their behavior and choices. Other times we gather information, interpret the facts and create paths of action that we hope will result in desired outcomes. On occasion, we do whatever comes most naturally, most easily, or that which we have always done, hoping that these choices will provide the satisfaction we seek.

Often, however, we take cues from leaders – that is, from individuals who describe a preferable future in which we can participate and add value. That future possibility, known as vision, gives us a sense of hope and meaning as well as a direction to pursue. The leader is the individual who keeps us excited about and focused upon that vision, and gives us a group with which may align ourselves to corporately seek meaning, fulfillment, belonging and impact.

Unfortunately, most of us have bought into an unhealthy understanding of leadership. We have been taught that leadership is about one individual performing all of the critical tasks – motivating, mobilizing, directing and resourcing people to fulfill a vision – at a level of excellence and influence that separates him/her from the bulk of humanity. The combination of skills and abilities required to be a great leader has caused many people to lament the absence of leaders in our society.

Let me provide some evidence of why I contend that we have unrealistic expectations for our leaders. In a nationwide survey we conducted among 1005 adults, people identified those things they feel are "very important" for a leader to do. Here is the profile.

87% expect leaders to motivate people to get involved in meaningful causes and activity

78% believe leaders should negotiate compromises and resolve conflicts when they arise

77% look to leaders to determine and convey the course of action that people should take in order to produce desirable conditions and outcomes

76% rely on leaders to identify and implement courses of action that are in the best interests of society, even if some of those choices are unpopular

75% expect leaders to invest their time and energy in training more leaders who will help bring the vision to reality

63% want leaders to communicate vision so that they know where things are headed and what it will take to get there

61% say that leaders are responsible for the directing and production of employees associated with the leader's organization or cause

61% think that leaders should analyze situations and create the strategies and plans that direct the resources of those who follow them

56% hold leaders responsible for managing the day-to-day details of the operation[1]

The list goes on, but the point is that we have developed an unreasonable notion of what a leader should do. Look at the breadth of tasks and abilities demanded by the expectations reflected in that list – and, of course, realize that there are additional expectations that the typical person holds of leaders beyond those listed here. Who could possibly meet such a range of disparate expectations? People expect the central leader to direct activity, encourage participants, supply resources, evaluate plans and progress, motivate participants, negotiate agreements, strategize, manage people, reinforce commitments, recruit necessary colleagues, communicate conditions, plans and assignments, train leaders, resolve conflicts, and so on.

Set Up for Failure

Would you agree that a person would have to be super-human to accomplish all of this? Amazingly, that's what we expect a leader to do. No wonder we are consistently disappointed by the leaders who held such promise before they assumed positions of significant authority and responsibility. Our surveys have shown that during the past two decades there has been a continual decline in satisfaction with leadership in churches, government, non-profits, schools, businesses and families.

When you reach a point of frustration or incapacity, one useful strategy is to go back and question your assumptions to determine if they are errant and therefore contributing to the blockage. If we take that approach in relation to our consternation regarding leadership, we will most likely conclude that the real problem is not our leaders but the unhealthy expectations we have of them. Few people have the individual capacity to deliver all that we have come to expect of those in positions of authority. We set leaders up for failure by holding them to absurd performance standards. We set organizations up for failure by intimately tying the success and well-being of the institution to the quality of leadership it receives. We set people up for frustration, disappointment and failure by basing their present and future well-being upon the capacity of the individual leader whom they most closely follow in any given dimension of their life.

Once we understand this situation and decide to examine the alternatives available to improve matters, there are several options we may consider.

First, we could accept this situation as a reality that is certainly imperfect but one that cannot and will not change. From that perspective, our responsibility is to simply make the best of the situation. No matter how many superior scenarios we might dream up, they are not likely to become reality, so we might as well not tantalize ourselves with unrealistic potentials. Our best response would be to deal with reality. While such an analysis may have some appeal, it is undoubtedly a defeatist, lazy-minded perspective. It is hard to imagine any scenario in life in which improvements are impossible.

A second option would be to assume that the real problem has been our failure to identify the most qualified leaders – and that if we can get those people in place, things will get better. This is a common complaint heard within the political arena: the system and the election process scares away the most capable and qualified candidates, leaving us with those who are so desperate for the job that they will do whatever it takes to win elected office. Once again, this view is not very realistic. True leaders rarely shrink from a reasonable challenge, especially if one of the outcomes they might achieve is changing the system to facilitate better outcomes and to make it more attractive to other leaders.

Third, we might posit that past and present leaders have failed to meet our expectations because they have not been adequately trained. This notion is undermined by ample evidence that suggests our leaders often receive the best training available, whether that is from schools, in the field or through mentoring. Effective leaders have many traits, and among those are a desire to succeed – which often drives them to gain the training, information and skills needed to accomplish their goals. While there are many examples that we could site of leaders not having enough training, it does not appear that this explanation is sufficient to describe the existing dearth of effective leaders, especially in our churches.

A final alternative would be to accept the fact that the current system does not work because it has an inherent flaw in its foundation. Such broad thinking opens up a world of possibilities and conjecture. What hypotheses are worth testing? If we were to build the "ideal model" of leadership, regardless of what models now prevail, what would that model look like? Working backwards from a clear-cut notion of "effective leadership," what would we strive to facilitate? In other words, rather than try to enable existing leaders to live up to the extremely high levels of performance we demand of them, how could we reconceptualize and innovatively redefine the leadership process?

Teams to the Rescue

Let me confess that it took me a long time to realize that the first three perspectives described above – that is, learning to live with things as they are, recruiting better quality people, and providing people with better training – will not produce the results that we are seeking. As a product of the institutions and methods that produced the problem in the first place, I had been completely blinded to alternatives to the leader-as-superstar approach.

Over the past two years I have had the privilege of discovering what many other people already knew and practiced: leadership works best when it is provided by *teams* of gifted *leaders* serving together in pursuit of a clear and compelling vision.

In the past decade there have been more than 4,000 new books written about leadership. Most of them discuss the indispensable skills needed to become king of the hill; few of them downplay the importance of personal superiority in favor of serving within a team context. Almost every leadership book talks about what the central leader can do to satisfy people's demands and outperform everyone else; rarely do leadership books or training courses dare to suggest that leadership is best accomplished without a high-profile, multi-talented, popular icon in the center-stage spotlight. But we have found that the "superstar" model of leadership, while appealing and not without some experiential validity, can do more to decimate the health of an organization than to facilitate its well-being.

After spending years conducting and analyzing research for government agencies, political leaders, Fortune 500 corporations, non-profit organizations and churches, I am convinced that the greatest challenges in our society stem from the absence of great leadership. We live in an increasingly complex and sophisticated society. People are constantly bombarded by opportunities, challenges and choices. No one can deny that we do, indeed, live in the land and age of opportunity.

But as human beings, we are prone to chasing outcomes that may not be realistic or even in our own best interests. Often we ignore the common good for the personal good. As often as not we make choices that we later regret, or that reflect poor judgment. Making good choices, discerning appropriate priorities, staying focused and on-track is exceedingly difficult. What will enable us to make progress toward outcomes that honor God, improve people's quality of life, and facilitate joy and meaning?

Leadership.

But the answer does not lie in unearthing more of the superhero leaders who satisfy the grandiose, ever-expanding demands of the people. The answer lies in combining the talents of gifted leaders to create synergistic outcomes. Team leadership is the only approach that carries the promise of satisfying the needs of our society. Solo leaders will always have an important place in our present and future reality, but teams hold the key to the future.

The Impact
of Team Leadership

In conversations with people, I have come to realize that we are not aware of just how much our lives have been impacted by leadership teams. Consider just a few examples that you may not have considered.

- Major political decisions are made at both the state and federal levels by executives whom we have elected – specifically, by the President of the U.S. and by the Governor of your state. But do you realize that those two individuals, while elected to lead, rely heavily upon a cabinet – a small group of advisors who are leaders and provide substantial input into the key strategic decisions made by the chief executive? It is the rare – and, usually, unsuccessful – government leader who makes important, life-impacting decisions

13

without careful study and discussion among a handful of selected counselors whose experience, skills and abilities complement those of the chief executive.

- Your physical safety has been sustained by the military. You may be aware that key military decisions are rarely the choice of one individual, such as a General, but are the outcome of a small group of experienced, trained professionals who work together to make important decisions. At the policy-making level, we might identify the Joint Chiefs of Staff as such a leadership team. Within a given branch of the military there are other teams at work, enabling the chief leader of the branch to make significant decisions.

- Sports teams use multiple leaders to devise effective strategy, representing a team behind the scenes as well as the team that you enjoy watching on the field. In football, the head coach works with a coaching team that usually includes a defensive coach, an offensive coach, a coach of special teams (kick returns, kickoff teams, etc.) and a tactician who has studied the opponent to understand their strengths and weaknesses. In basketball you may have the head coach working in tandem with a coach of the guards, one who focuses on the forwards and centers, plus another who tracks what the opponents have been doing. Baseball teams have coaches who help the manager by focusing on various functions, such as hitting, pitching, scouting and conditioning.

- The board of directors of many large corporations use an "executive committee" that shapes policy and other core decisions for the corporation. That committee is usually a handful of people – from three to seven individuals – who assist the board chairperson in developing key outcomes. The team often encompasses individuals who possess divergent, complementary backgrounds, covering areas such as finance, human resources, management, marketing and technology.

Clearly, our lives are affected by teams every day. In many cases, we may not realize the depth and range of leadership competence provided simply because the team works so smoothly – almost as if it were one indivisible entity, rather than a collection of individuals. In these situations, the team embraces one unified position, speaks with one voice, gains a single image in the public's eye, and operates with such unity that we remain unaware of the multiple parts that work cooperatively behind the scenes. When those parts are working in lock-step, all we see – or care about – are the results. A major advantage of being led by a team is that the results almost always transcend what any individual or two people from that team could have produced without the assistance of the other leaders involved in that team.

Challenges for Leaders

To sense the full impact of the importance of shifting from solo leadership to team leadership, take a moment to consider some of the challenges that face our culture today. In brief, those include the following:

- Population growth: already the third most populated nation in the world, the U.S. will add another 30 million people to its body this decade – roughly the equivalent of adding the same number of people as live in our most populated state, California. That growth will result in new pressures, needs, and expectations.

- Morality: one of the growing concerns of Americans is the moral and ethical decay of our nation. In a previous book I predicted that this would be the decade in which America would be overtaken by moral anarchy – an environment in which people do whatever they feel is in their personal interests, regardless of the law, the common good or the needs of the groups with which they are associated. While a remnant is concerned about moral decline, most people accept it and strive to cope with it – primarily by honing their own decadent practices.

- Expectations: people expect to have the best of everything, at low-cost, delivered immediately. Having abandoned God as the center of our lives, we seek fulfillment from other sources, especially our material possessions and entertainment experiences. We resent anything that gets in the way of being able to achieve maximum pleasure.

- Families: with divorce commonplace, the introduction of "gay marriages," legal abortions, euthanasia being practiced, latchkey children, family poverty at high levels, in-home violence growing, births outside of marriage at record levels, working mothers as the norm, and the declining quality of communication within families, relying upon the family to be the primary delivery agent of appropriate values and behavior is a pipe dream. Families themselves no longer turn inward for the direction and resources they need for maturation and quality of life, but now they turn outward to get what they need.

- Values: traditional values such as absolute moral truth, personal integrity and respect for authority have all been twisted beyond recognition. The new values that are in place have reshaped our relationships with people and institutions.

Once again, the list of challenges facing leaders could go on for pages. (In a book being published concurrent to this one – *Boiling Point* – I spend 300-plus pages detailing the changing nature of our society and its implications for leaders and churches.)[2] The point is that the severity of the cultural shifts we have witnessed in recent years has emphasized that one person is not likely to provide the breadth and acuity of leadership demanded by such an environment. Expecting any individual to meet such extraordinary demands borders on being cruel and unjust.

Leadership Changes in the Church

We could continue our examination of the context in which leadership occurs by studying some of the shifts happening in churches.

Again, consider the following handful of trends that are reshaping what leadership in ministry looks like today.

1. Increasing numbers of Senior Pastors are shifting from being a preacher-counselor to a leader-trainer. Without diminishing the importance of preaching and teaching there is a heightened realization that the congregation relies upon the Senior Pastor for vision, motivation and mobilization. The result is a redefining of how pastors use their resources to have impact.

2. Four forces are converging to change the role of the laity in leadership. First, people are demanding participation in the development of their current experience and future conditions. Second, Christians are becoming more aware of their spiritual gifts – and desirous of using those gifts in personal ministry and for the benefit of their church. Third, seminaries are not producing leaders, requiring churches to look elsewhere for individuals who have been called by God to lead, have been trained to do so and have leadership experience. Fourth, pastors are increasingly open to sharing the leadership of the church's ministry with competent and committed laity. The outgrowth of these new realities is that churches are identifying, training and deploying congregants as key leaders within the ministry. Pastors, staff members and preachers are increasingly being promoted from within the congregation instead of from resumes presented by outsiders.

3. Few churches do a good job of determining success in ministry. One trend that may help to overcome that disability is the transition from thinking about church growth, which is primarily quantitative in nature, to focusing upon church health, which addresses ministry quality. This change in emphasis will necessarily demand a different leadership focus and new skills.

4. In the past decade, the Holy Spirit has received greater attention and devotion than at any time in the past half century. One implication of this "comeback" by the Third Person of the Trinity is that church leaders must now consider the appropriate blending of business-oriented skills with sensitivity to the promptings of the Holy Spirit.

This produces a better balance of head and heart in leading the ministry.

5. More than three decades of extensive research has confirmed the view that although leadership skills can be taught, leadership will always be an art, not a definable science. As such, while methodology is important and techniques can be taught to bring about superior outcomes, the acceptance of leadership as a "soft science" frees churches and practitioners to concentrate on leadership as a ministry, rather than a discipline that facilitates ministry. The bottom line is that leaders minister by serving others.

6. Congregants demand excellence and relevance from their church. This perspective has also changed the way in which they want to be treated when they invest themselves in ministry. Rather than being described as volunteers, churches are discovering that people need to be treated as ministry professionals. Churches are changing the terms they use to describe volunteers, the quantity of resources made available to them, and are providing different forms of supervision to these ministry partners. This alters how full-time church leaders perceive and carry out their work within the congregational context.

Each of these trends points to a meaningful shift in how people think, interact, work and perceive ministry. When the context changes, leadership must adapt. The changes described above demand that leaders perform the same fundamental functions – giving people a sense of where to go and how to get there – but to deliver the related resources in ways that fit the new cultural context.

Pastors' Self-Perceptions

Consider another key insight from our research: most pastors neither see themselves as leaders, nor aspire to be leaders. In a recent national survey of Protestant Senior Pastors, we asked them to identify their spiritual gifts. Only 12% of the pastors – that's about one out of every eight – said they have the gift of leadership.

In contrast, two-thirds of all pastors said they have the gift of teaching or preaching. They have accurately recognized that teaching and leading are two very distinct responsibilities and activities, requiring different skills that produce differing results. The prevailing mind set among most pastors is that their primary job is to preach from the Bible and provide opportunities for teaching and caring (e.g., worship services, Sunday school classes). Our studies have shown that there is a very high level of frustration among most pastors: they went to seminary to learn how to preach and pastor – not how to lead – yet people expect strong, visionary leadership.

Another relevant finding from research we conducted several years ago is that less than one out of every twenty Senior Pastors can articulate the vision for the ministry he/she leads. Combine the personal conviction that they have not been called to lead with the inability to articulate God's vision for their ministry and you can clearly see that if we rely upon the Senior Pastors of our country's Protestant churches to provide all or most of the leadership in our churches, we will be in trouble. A church can compensate for the absence of many skills and resources, but it cannot overcome the absence of effective leadership. If that leadership is not going to come from pastors, then it must come from somewhere else.

And that is where the practice of team leadership enters the picture.

FOOTNOTES

[1] This survey was a nationwide, random sample survey of 1005 adults conducted in July, 1996 by the Barna Research Group, Ltd.

[2] This book discusses the social and spiritual trends and responses that characterize America, including our predictions of what the country will be like at the end of this decade. We have endeavored to describe the implications of these changes and how Christians might reasonably respond to these challenges. See George Barna and Mark Hatch, *Boiling Point*, Ventura, CA: Regal Books, 2001.

CHAPTER TWO

BASIC CONTOURS
OF TEAM LEADERSHIP

Even though leadership plays such an integral role in every person's life, we throw the words "leader" and "leadership" around quite carelessly. Often you hear someone referred to as "a leader in her field" only to discover that the person is not a leader of people so much as she is a well-known or popular individual. Mary Higgins Clark sells millions of novels, but that does not make her a leader in the field of fiction writing. Glen Rice scores a lot of points for the Knicks, but that does not make him the team leader.

The Heart of Leadership

Leadership is more than calling the shots, and it is more than merely having influence on people's thoughts and behavior. Similarly, holding a position or title that implies a person is a leader bears little relationship to whether or not, in reality, the person is one. Neither possessing a charismatic personality nor massive intellect makes a person a leader.

Leadership is about calling, character and competencies – a complete package of components that enables a leader to help people to reach their goals and potential. By focusing on the will of God and the needs of His creation, a leader is ultimately a servant. It is only by encouraging, empowering, enforcing and evaluating that a leader assists people in their quest to achieve meaning and fulfillment in life. In other words, a leader succeeds only if his/her followers succeed, and the followers succeed only if their leader is sensitive and responsive to God and empowers the people to do His will.

21

To lead people means that you motivate, mobilize, direct and resource them so that they are able to fulfill a vision that they have agreed is appropriate and worthy of their pursuit.[1] But perhaps the definition of leadership raises a question in your mind: who can do all of that with excellence, especially in a broad and complicated environment?

Let me broach the topic from a different angle. One of the most common complaints I hear from pastors is that they want lay people to be involved as leaders in ministry, but they simply cannot find enough qualified and competent people to fill the various leaderships posts that exist within their ministry. Frankly, if they are seeking out a score of dynamic, charismatic, articulate, multi-talented individuals who will provide outstanding direction and support to church people, they are right. We do not have enough of those people to get the job done.

However, God never sets us up for failure; He always provides His people with whatever resources they need, when they need them, to accomplish His will. The fact that churches do not have a plentiful source of high-powered, intelligent, aggressive, super-competent, highly-regarded, productive leaders is not because God has forgotten what we need in order to faithfully and effectively serve Him. God never intended for any church to have an adequate supply of those types of people because He never intended for us to dessert the leadership model that He provided to us – that is, the model of team leadership.

Redefining Ministry Leadership

In my research with churches across the nation, I have recognized two realities: leadership is indispensable to ministry success (defined as consistent and widespread life transformation) and we expect too much of individual leaders.

In other words, what may seem like a contradiction – i.e., that God expects leaders to facilitate the pursuit and fulfillment of the vision He gives them, yet He does not provide many individuals whose leadership capabilities are of an extraordinary caliber – is not really a contradiction after all. The problem is not that we do not have enough good leaders, but that we have an errant expectation about what a leader is called to do.

God, with characteristic grace and wisdom, has provided us with all the resources we need to accomplish His ends on earth. He has even provided us with the leadership talent pool that we may draw from – if we know what we're looking for. If you think about Jesus' disciples, it doesn't take long to realize that few of them seemed like the kind of strong, visionary, world-changing kinds of leaders that we seek as the senior pastor of churches these days. Instead, He used individuals who were gifted, capable leaders requiring training and vision.

The story of the Church, as depicted in the Book of Acts, is the tale of a community of faith that is directed by a team of leaders working together toward a common vision. Had the Church relied upon a single, incredibly gifted, magnetic individual to replace Jesus, the Church would surely have collapsed. What the disciples discovered was that none of them had the complete package of gifts, abilities and insights necessary to facilitate the growth of the Christian Church – but that each had a very significant and defined role to play in that revolutionary undertaking.

We often think of our age and our tools as the most sophisticated in human history. Perhaps that is true. But one other reality is also true: "there is nothing new under the sun." (Ecclesiastes 1:9) Throughout history, people have benefited from having teams of leaders that provided the direction they needed. We may read stories about individual leaders who were unusually gifted and capable, but those people are the exception to the rule. Much of the great leadership delivered throughout the ages has come from teams, even if the public's sense of that guidance was largely related to one person's performance.

Is yours a team-led church?

What Is A Team?

Most churches employ two types of gatherings that are assembled for productive purposes: work groups and committees. **Work groups** are collections of people who come together for a particular duration to accomplish a specific task. The task is not necessarily related to a vision, and the group's focus might not be the future. A work group generally does not have the special combination of spiritual gifts and natural talents required to accomplish a plethora of outcomes that move the church toward the fulfillment of God's vision. A **committee** is a collection of individuals who meet for discussion and, perhaps, to make recommendations regarding policy, programs or plans. Committees typically have little, if any, authority to act. Often, they provide the organization that joined them together with ideas, preferences or suggestions that a leadership body then considers and passes judgment upon.

A **leadership team** is quite different. It is a small group of leaders who possess complementary gifts and skills, are committed to each other's growth and success while leading a larger group of people in pursuing a common vision, specific performance goals and a plan of action, and who will hold themselves mutually accountable. Let's explore each of those components.

Small group. A large group cannot lead. Anyone who has been involved in effective leadership knows that once a group gets beyond five people or so, it becomes unwieldy and degenerates into compromises that satisfy the lowest common denominator. At that stage, the focus of the group is not upon a commonly-held vision but upon producing some tangible outcome with which everyone is comfortable. That is not leadership; that is accommodation. Effective leadership teams typically have three to five people. Less than three leaves you without the horsepower to get the job done. More than five produces inefficiencies and excessive compromise.

Leaders. A leadership team is a collection of leaders – not warm bodies willing to help out, not people with titles, but individuals who possess the calling, character and competencies that qualify them as leaders. Since the very purpose of the team is to provide leadership, it must contain individuals who have the capacity to lead. Further, the notion of leaders implies that there are followers, too. A leadership team is of no significance unless it is helping followers to accomplish the vision.

Complementary gifts and skills. One of the most important attributes of effective leadership teams is that the leaders have a combination of gifts and skills that complement each other. One of the worst imaginable scenarios is to have three or four people with identical gifts and talents working in a team: you will experience tension and conflict of world-class proportions! A team is effective when the four leadership aptitudes are fully and broadly represented among the team members. (We will discuss leadership aptitudes in chapter 5.)

Committed to each other. In a true team, the leaders are committed to each other's growth and success in ministry. Granted, these individuals may not become best friends, but they must respect each other and care about the personal maturation of each other. Unless the team members experience such continual growth, the team will suffer. Because a team is an expression of community, mutual concern is an indispensable ingredient in the team dynamic. A team in which the members are *not* committed to each other is a team that may produce some desirable results, but it is not likely to exhaust its potential as a team.

Common vision. It is the vision that brings the team together and facilitates their passion to move forward in tandem. The vision unites and excites those who wish to be part of the process. The vision serves as the filter through which efforts are examined: success is defined by progress made toward fulfilling the vision. The vision is the core concept that the team communicates to the population it is leading. Not only must the team be united in its acceptance of, and devotion to the vision, but unless the team can inspire others to own the vision, the team will fail in its efforts.

Goals and plan. A vision that has no goals and plans associated with it is merely a fantasy. Leaders must move toward the vision by identifying realistic and measurable goals, and then facilitating the development of specific courses of action that will produce the required outcomes. A team without goals and plans is a social club.

Mutually accountable. One of the distinctives of leadership teams is their determination to evaluate their own efforts and to enable each other to live up to specific standards – both team standards and individual standards. One reason why leaders fall into disgrace is because they do not have people who know them and whom they trust to bring them into accountability. Great teams are comprised of leaders who have developed sufficient trust, rapport and vulnerability to keep each other honest, focused, productive, humble and inspired.

When these seven elements are combined, the result is a powerful assembly of individuals whose ability to serve people is multiplied beyond what any one of them could possibly have accomplished alone. Teams make mistakes, sometimes they lose their way, and occasionally they dissipate in personality snits or other unfortunate conflicts. More often than not, though, leaders love working in teams and are ecstatic about the outcomes of the team's efforts.

Clergy As Team Leaders
in Larger Churches

Less than 2% of America's Protestant churches attract 1000 or more adults each weekend; less than one out of every seven have attendance exceeding 600 people in a typical week. Yet, despite their relative scarcity in the church landscape, large churches have enormous influence in the church marketplace. Having reached a different scale of ministry, are large churches exempt from the necessity of utilizing team leadership?

Our study found just the opposite to be the case: a large church that does not use teams will suffer. Specifically, its leaders will be burned out; its capacity to minister effectively will be limited; the senior pastor will either become a cult hero or blockage in the ministry process; and the ministry will become less participative. The larger the church gets, the more imperative it becomes for the ministry to rely upon team leadership to remain healthy. The process operates best when the clergy in a church create and minister within a team culture. The larger a church becomes, the greater the number of "directors" that are added to the staff. It is imperative for all of the full-time professionals to serve as team leaders, not solo practitioners. Not only is the ministry output more significant when staff work as team, but their cooperative effort models true team-work for the laity. The result is greater ministry satisfaction among the clergy, a better teaching process for lay leaders, and heightened transformational capacity.

Team Leadership in the Small Church

While most pastors aspire to lead large churches, the reality is that a majority of American churches have fewer than 100 adults attending on any given weekend. Less than one out of five have more than one full-time professional on the church payroll. In other words, most churches are the equivalent of a sole proprietorship – a soul pastorship, maybe? – that might appear to preclude such churches from involving the pastor in team leadership. Indeed, the fact that a huge majority of churches do not have more than one or two ministry professionals on the payroll emphasizes two importance conditions: the necessity of laity being involved in leadership, and the significance of teams as the leadership framework.

Once again, our research shows that not only can teams work in a small church environment, but that the better they work, the more likely it is that the church will not remain small for long. When leaders combine their efforts with those of others who possess complementary gifts, that mixture is likely to boost the impact of the church within the community and attract many curious people – some of whom will be impressed enough to stay and add their efforts to the ministry mix. As in any other scenario, the pastor must lead the way, but he/she must do so by being a team player – a leader of leaders, certainly, but also a colleague in ministry serving in harmony with the contingent of leaders God has brought to the church.

Those who criticize the Church for the consumer mentality of Christians often miss the boat – not because they find fault with the consumption of religious resources by church-goers, but because they fail to take their complaints deep enough to understand the roots of the problem. Many church-goers have no choice but to *consume* ministry because they are not invited and prepared to *do* ministry – especially if they are gifted as leaders. The desire to somehow engage in spiritual activity moves millions of individuals to settle for watching ministry rather than engaging in ministry. The passive observation of ministry is a reflection of pastors who reject the prospects of impact afforded through team leadership. Instead, tens of thousands of pastors "protect" the church's ministry by waiting for the "right" person to come along who can provide compelling, irresistible, multi-faceted leadership. Of course, such a person rarely comes along, leaving the church dissipated by dashed hopes, missed opportunities and depressed progress.

In the meantime, by excluding lay leaders from exercising their gifts and abilities, the church becomes just another example of professional service delivery: trained and certified professionals (i.e., clergy) providing the goods and services (e.g., worship events, classes) needed or desired by consumers (aka congregants). The ministry's potential is therefore limited by the capacity of the professionals on the payroll.

Rejecting team leadership essentially ignores biblical precedent and principles. Believers are entrusted with specials abilities (i.e., spiritual gifts) so that they may serve people more effectively. Preventing people from using those gifts diminishes the joy of ministry and reduces the health of the church. Conversely, identifying just a handful of leadership superstars to carry the church sets up those individuals for failure and frustration. In fact, by emphasizing solo leadership, we inadvertently focus on what we accomplish, based on our unique talents and stellar efforts, rather than focusing upon God, and what He is able to accomplish through us via the empowerment of His Holy Spirit. Ministry leadership is not the exclusive domain of clergy, but a discipline to be practiced by all of those whom God has called and equipped for the function of leading the Church. If effective leadership is going to take place in churches, it will be largely because lay people are using their leadership abilities.

The Bible and Teams

I sometimes cringe when I read an impassioned plea for Christians or churches to adopt a particular perspective or practice because it is biblical, only to find the scriptural evidence to be forced. Let me be forthright about the role of teams in the Bible: the Word does not make a big deal about the importance of leaders serving in teams. Most of the wisdom gleaned regarding teams must be drawn from passages or stories in which the key principles relate to other aspects of life and ministry. In fact, while I believe the Bible is a great text on leadership, it directly discusses leadership in relatively few passages; most leadership principles derived from the Bible are inferential.

With this caveat in mind, let me suggest a few ways in which the Bible endorses the value and significance of team-based leadership.

Moses

Moses was a fascinating leader. Reluctant to lead from the start, he learned many leadership lessons the hard way. Two elements stick out in my mind about Moses and his involvement with teams. First, he clearly recognized that while God called him to lead, he was hampered by severe limitations and was reticent to take on such responsibility. His reaction was to ask God to provide him with colleagues who could compensate for his overt weaknesses – that is, to let him lead as part of a team, in which he would (by God's design) serve as the Directing Leader, and the captain of the team. In response, God provided two leaders to share the burden: Aaron and Joshua.

The second insight relates to the potential inefficiencies of solo leadership. Even though Moses had capable teammates, he retained much of the responsibility for directing the people, making public policy and supervising the operations of their venture. In Exodus 18, Moses' father-in-law, Jethro, pays Moses and his family a visit. He observes Moses' typical work day and is appalled by the bottleneck Moses had created by striving to be all things to all people. Jethro offered some simple advice; divide the leadership duties into manageable portions and delegate some of the responsibility to other gifted servants. That advice changed Moses' life, freeing him to focus on aspects of directing the nation that only he could perform. Solo leadership can only take you as far as the capacity of the individual; increasing the leadership capacity by using a team enhances the quality of life for the people as well as for their leader.

Nehemiah

Throughout his campaign to restore the city walls, Nehemiah relied heavily upon teams of gifted individuals with complementary skills to facilitate the fulfillment of the vision God had given to him. At different times throughout the campaign he organized different teams for divergent purposes. The walls would never have been built if he had relied upon a more traditional style of one-man leadership.

Jesus

Doesn't it seem most sensible that to accomplish a spiritual end, Jesus would have turned to the people most interested in spirituality, i.e., the religious leaders of the day? And wouldn't you expect Him, given a limit of barely three years in public ministry, to pursue alliances with high-profile individuals whose resumes proved that they knew how to lead effectively? As usual, He broke all the rules. He called upon a group of uneducated, low-key, ill-trained individuals whose character seemed pretty solid, and who were willing to sacrifice whatever they had to in order to be apprentices to the master leader. Clearly, Jesus' intent was not to raise up eleven future hot shots whose stellar performances would wow the world, but rather to prepare a humble group whose limitations would force them to work together to complete the assignment He had given to them while remaining focused on Him. Jesus was training teams of leaders, not potential members of the Future CEO Club.

Paul

On his missionary journeys the most prolific of the apostles always traveled and ministered with a team. Whether it was in the company of Barnabas, John, Simeon, Lucius and Manaen (Acts 13), serving with Timothy, Judas and Silas (Acts 15-16), or ministering alongside of various combinations of other leaders, Paul was the quintessential team player. His passage in Ephesians (4:12) remains one of the central challenges to the Church to train laity to do the entire work of the ministry. His entries regarding spiritual gifts (1 Corinthians 12 and Romans 12) not only identify leadership as a core gift, but further suggest that rather than focus on one individual who can do it all, God's intent was to prepare each of us to be a role player, not a superhero.

There are other Bible passages in both the Old and New Testaments that also address the importance of leadership provided through teams of gifted individuals. The point is not to diminish the value of individual leaders but simply to recognize that the Bible does acknowledge teams as a viable leadership strategy.

My passion is for God's leaders to express their leadership calling, character and competencies within the optimal environment to be unleashed and utilized for the advancement of His kingdom. In some situations that will mean solo leadership; in others, the optimal approach is to lead in a team-based environment. The longer we deny the benefits of team leadership, the less likely it is that we will experience the power of God in the Church, in society and in our personal experience. There is only one ministry superstar – Jesus Christ. If we persist in seeking to lead churches through the display of talents and abilities resident within a few unusually capable individuals, rather than allowing the community of believers to use their significant but less captivating leadership skills in an orchestrated unison to accomplish synergistic outcomes, the Church and our society will pay the price for such defiance.

FOOTNOTES

[1] Vision is a clear and compelling mental portrait of a preferable future that God communicates to His chosen people. Vision is about change, purpose, focus, and obedience to God. Without vision, there is no leadership. For Christians, one of the challenges is to pursue God's vision, not a person's own vision for the future. A leader is successful when he/she is effectively enabling people to pursue (and, ultimately, fulfill) the vision entrusted to the people by God.

CHAPTER THREE

WITHOUT VISION, THERE IS NO LEADERSHIP

Vision is to a leader as air is to a human being: without it, you die. The leaders of a church must have a clear and motivating grasp of God's vision for their ministry; the leaders working together in a team must possess a firm understanding of His vision for their team, as it fits within the encompassing vision of the church in which they serve.

The concept of vision is thousands of years old. It has shaped cultures for centuries and centuries and has touched the lives of people on every continent of the globe. Consider some of the historical statements about vision.

God inspired Solomon to write Proverbs 29:18, concerning the centrality of vision. "Where there is no vision, the people perish" is the King James rendition; the New International Version interprets the passage as "Where there is no revelation, the people cast off restraint." My favorite interpretation of this verse is from the Living Bible: "Where there is ignorance of God, the people run wild." Vision is the concept that comes from God Himself to keep His people focused, under control and devoted to endeavors that are meaningful to them and Him.

An ancient Chinese proverb admonishes people to devote themselves to what is most important – and to discern that by thinking circumspectly about the future. "If your vision is for one year, plant wheat. If your vision is for a decade, plant trees. If your vision is for a lifetime, plant people." Ideally, vision is not for the short term.

Great artists are people of vision; through their art they create something beautiful or meaningful out of nothing. The renowned Italian artist Michelangelo prayed that God would keep his vision alive. "Lord, grant that I may always desire to do more than I am able to accomplish." Vision, the concept of what does not exist but could, is what motivates us to continue to strive toward the fulfillment of that outcome.

Pastor and civil rights activist Martin Luther King, Jr. challenged his followers to commit themselves to a worthy vision. "If a man hasn't discovered something he will die for, he isn't fit to live." That "something" alluded to by Dr. King was God's vision. For him, it was a world in which racial discrimination was nowhere to be found, where love reigned supreme and overcame all distinctions and inequalities based on race, creed, or background.

God has a unique vision for your church. He has a significant vision for each ministry within your church. These visions are provided to His called, gifted leaders for the purpose of strategically directing the resources of the church. Grasping, casting and indefatigably pursuing God's vision is the central, defining characteristic of God's leaders. It is the commitment to that vision, and our capacity to bring it to fruition, that dictates the shape of the Church and the depth of influence that the Church has on the world.

Why is vision so critical to leadership? Simply put, if you cannot articulate a clear picture of what you are seeking to achieve, how can you lead people there? Since a leader must motivate, mobilize and direct people, on what basis would you accomplish such outcomes without casting a compelling vision? At the most basic level, realize that a leader is taking people somewhere. Without vision, where would you lead them?

Therein lies one of the secrets to why churches are not having the impact that they could. Great leadership lies at the heart of every successful ministry. Vision is at the heart of great leadership. Many churches struggle either because people who aren't leaders lead them or they have leaders who do not possess God's vision for their ministry.[1]

Without leaders who hold a firm understanding of God's vision for their ministry, the entire church suffers.

- Vision inspires people by providing them with hope, meaning and significant challenges; the absence of vision robs them of inspiration.

- Vision attracts people to a cause by giving them something worth investing in and something to focus upon that transcends the mundane endeavors of daily life; the absence of vision relegates them to a life of insignificance and disengagement from things that have eternal meaning.

- Vision builds community by providing people a common purpose and putting our natural competitiveness and pettiness in perspective; the absence of vision prevents us from building life changing relationships and diminishing our tendency to see the worst in others.

- Vision sustains people by giving them a compelling reason to persevere and to stay focused on what really matters; the absence of vision facilitates majoring on the minors.

Perspective in Ministry

There are three significant concepts that relate to the nature and perspective of your ministry. Those concepts are mission, vision and values. What are these concepts? How do they work together in a church?[2]

35

Mission describes your overall purpose for existence. When you describe your mission to someone, you define for them the most fundamental understanding of what you are striving to accomplish. Mission represents a broad stroke portrait of your life or ministry. The mission of a church is to facilitate meaningful worship, evangelism, discipleship, service, stewardship and fellowship – or, more succinctly, to facilitate life transformation through which people become evermore like Jesus Christ. The mission of an evangelist is to win souls to Christ. The mission of a leader is to motivate, mobilize, resource and direct people to fulfill a vision.

Every Christian church has the same mission as every other Christian church. Every Christian evangelist has the same mission as every other Christian evangelist. Every leader in Christian ministry has the same mission as every other leader in Christian ministry. They exist to see similar outcomes happen – and yet each is not interchangeable with the other. That's where vision comes into the picture.

Vision is focused guidance that helps you determine the unique way in which you have been called to fulfill the mission. Mission without vision leads to complete frustration and paralysis because it can never be completed or perfectly fulfilled – it is too general and too broad. Vision is the idiosyncratic way in which God wants to use you to complete a part of the grand puzzle of the development of His kingdom. Mission is too generic to point you in a specific direction; vision is the concept that tells you what you should do, in specific ways, to produce results that honor God by fulfilling the special role He has carved out for you.

Values play an important role in this process, too. Values are the principles and standards that define what is right, desirable and worthwhile. Values relate to character, as experienced through a person's thoughts, words and behaviors. The values you possess constitute the non-negotiable outcomes of your being – the ways of living that are acceptable, appropriate and desirable from your frame of reference. Every individual lives in accordance with personal values, whether they have been articulated or not. In the same way, every church operates in concert with its values, whether they are clearly defined or latent.

In other words, mission is about participating in the purposes of His kingdom. Vision distills your small but necessary and unique role in doing so. Values provide the behavioral parameters that limit what you may and may not do in the process of pursuing the vision. These three notions, blended together into a coherent concept of reality, provide the directing perspective for your church or your life. Every church ought to identify its mission, vision and values so that people understand what it stands for, where it is going, and what is permissible in the process. Similarly, every Christian individual ought to identify his/her mission, vision and values for life and ministry, and use those insights to determine why to live, how to live, and where to minister. And, of course, every leader and leadership team must be able to articulate God's mission, vision and values for the leader and for the team, to provide a clear sense of how to make life and ministry glorifying to God, beneficial to the church, and personally meaningful and fulfilling.

Defining Vision More Specifically

As you strive to understand God's vision for your church, for your life, or for your team, think of it as a compelling mental portrait of a preferable future, communicated by God to His chosen leaders, based upon an accurate understanding of God, self and circumstances.

God's vision, whether it is for the organization (i.e., the church), the individual, or a team of individuals serving the organization (i.e., a leadership team within a church) is irresistible to those who have been called to partake in its pursuit. It is so personally exciting that it stimulates a deep desire to be involved in making it real. The concept itself is so real that you can see it clearly in your mind, just like a portrait painted for you by a renowned artist. The vision will be both exciting and unnerving, since it inevitably calls for change – but change from what exists to something indisputably superior. God's vision never rejects the past, but always builds a bridge from the past to the future.

He relies upon His chosen leaders to seek, grasp, communicate, and pursue His vision with vigor and diligence. That vision is the strategic fulfillment of the mission, but it must be operationalized if it is to be of any worth. This is accomplished by converting the concept of a preferable reality into a series of specific goals (i.e., measurable outcomes that relate to the mission, vision and values), strategies (i.e., general approaches designed to facilitate accomplishing the specified goals), and tactics (specific actions that relate to the strategies and undertaken to achieve specific goals).

Can you see the interrelatedness of these elements – and the distinctiveness of each? A ministry or team that operates solely on the basis of mission won't get very far because it has no real sense of direction, will see limited impact, and will lack the passion to sustain its efforts over time. A ministry or team that has never delineated its values will get into trouble because any behavior is justified by results – a philosophy that is antithetical to biblical Christianity. A ministry or team that strives to implement a vision without understanding the larger framework within which it fits, and without a connection to specified values, will be a task-oriented ministry that misses the mark.[3]

Getting Vision

Discerning God's vision for your life and ministry is between you and the Lord. If you have been called to lead others for the purposes of His kingdom, the vision will become the centerpiece of your ministry – the basis against which your ministry efforts should be judged, the motivation for continuing in the face of daunting challenges, the foundation of your attempts to enlist others in fulfilling the vision, and so forth. Because that vision is the core of what you relate to as a leader, or as a team, discerning the vision is one of the first tasks of a leader or team.

Identifying the vision is not necessarily easy, but it will produce multiple benefits in your life. Focusing on His vision as your direction in life and ministry will bring you closer to Him, give you strength and clarity regarding your life, increase your leadership influence, build your confidence in your ability to make good decisions, release you from the oppressive tyranny of making choices on the basis of feelings and politics, and enable you to eliminate distractions and diversions from your life without feeling guilty. Leaders pay a price for the privilege of leading God's people – just look at what Jesus, Moses, Paul and Peter went through as they sought to be faithful to God's vision for their life. But keep in mind that your personal investment in carrying out God's vision will pay off many times over in the end. There are several thousand years of recorded history among the people of God to support that claim.

Perhaps you're asking a very basic question at this point: how do you get God's vision? After years of study on this topic, including evaluations of how many of our most effective ministry leaders have arrived at a clarity regarding God's vision for them, it seems that the process itself is quite simple. I believe there are four steps involved.

First, you must know yourself inside out. That means understanding your personal strengths and weaknesses, your joys and fears, your past successes and failures, your character flaws, the spiritual gifts God has entrusted to you, your natural skills and abilities, and so on. All of these elements ultimately relate to who you are, how you relate to God, how He can use you, and what you must do to become the type of individual whom He can rely upon to do great things for His kingdom. You cannot be effective – or trusted – until you know yourself, because deep-rooted change will not occur until such a serious self-examination and personal spiritual enhancement process has been undertaken. God does not seek perfect people as leaders, but He does want people who are committed to serving Him as best they can. This self-assessment effort is critical in God being able to trust you with a vision of how and where to lead His people.

Second, you must know your ministry environment and the related opportunities. This entails three levels of examination. Naturally, you should have a firm understanding of the nature of your church: its mission, vision and values, along with the resident spiritual gifts, natural talents, physical resources, ministry opportunities, congregational history, and the like. Second, you need to know your community – its prevailing values, the most widespread felt needs, and people's life expectations. Finally, become intimately acquainted with your ministry colleagues. Get to know the leaders of other ministries in the area – their mission, vision and values, as well as their key programs, their successes and failures, their priorities, and their capabilities.

Third, you must know God. Of course, it is critical to have a deep, robust relationship with Him through prayer, worship, meditating on His Word and principles. Beyond that, you need to understand how He works- the nature of His character, how He interacts with leaders, the expectations He has for those leaders. These insights are gleaned from studying the Bible. You get to know Him in a more intimate way through prayer, meditation, fasting, solitude – the spiritual disciplines that enable you to supernaturally connect with the living God. These efforts will help you sharpen your focus on Him and draw you closer, which then facilitates the ability to understand what He is calling you to pursue.

Once you have committed yourself to the process of discerning the vision, it will take time to grasp God's ministry concept designed for you. Through a diligent regimen of prayer, reflection, Scripture study, examining your ministry context, and exploring the wisdom of trusted believers who know you and your ministry well, chances are good that the vision will be incrementally revealed to you. Before you run with it, the fourth step is to test it. Test it by getting feedback from the handful of intimate counselors whom you can trust, by evaluating the opened doors for ministry that coincide with your view of the vision, and by taking a step of faith to see what happens as you launch out toward fulfilling the vision. Be certain that you have His vision before you choose to broadcast that declaration to others.

In the discernment process, keep in mind that vision is not the result of consensus. What God wants does not rely upon a majority vote or some other democratic process. Man's ways are not God's ways, and we must be prepared to accept God's vision, even if it seems at odds with human wisdom. Committees, study commissions, denominational entities, and congregations are not the means through which God delivers His vision to a leader: He goes direct. This underscores why the capacity to understand and remain focused upon vision is one of the hallmarks of a leader.

God's vision often calls for us to achieve things we cannot, by human means, achieve – and that is His intent. If it were outcomes that we could accomplish without reliance upon Him, then the vision would defeat His desire to be in living partnership with us. Neither is His vision for us ever related or limited to numerical growth: He desires growth in character, exhibited through radical obedience and absolute commitment, regardless of how many people accept that challenge. The vision will be more specific than just devouring the Word, seeking souls, or worshiping Him – we're all called to do such basic acts of homage – and it will take more than just a few years to accomplish. Vision is for the long-term and it will probably take you a substantial period of time – months, perhaps even a year or two – to determine the vision.

Within the team context, realize that we are dealing with individual leaders, each of whom will have a personal vision from God for his/her life and ministry. Successful teams are those that bring together leaders driven by compatible visions. For instance, you might search for leaders who have vision related to discipleship, and let them discuss among themselves how they could work together to lead the church forward into a more effective and dynamic discipling ministry. Lay leaders whose passion is worship might find that their personal vision coincides perfectly with the vision that God entrusted to other leaders in the church regarding the ministry of worship. What emerges for the worship leadership team, then, is likely the result of a handful of leaders who share a passion for worship and find common ground in the vision with which God has empowered each of them.

Getting the Right Vision

A key point that has not yet been sufficiently emphasized is that the emergent vision must be God's, not ours. The tendency is for leaders to evaluate their resources and opportunities and develop a vision based on their own inclinations. This gets the church into trouble. Consider the differences between our vision and that provided to us by God.

For starters, human vision is quite limiting. We base our vision on what we can accomplish when we maximize our natural talents and skills. God's vision, however, pushes us beyond our capacity to achieve things than can only be ascribed to the work of the supernatural. God is not interested in what we can do; He is interested in what He can do through us, when we are willing vessels.

Typically, human vision is determined by that which brings us delight. After surveying the possibilities, we lean toward those outcomes that we find most appealing, exhilarating or exciting. The reason to pursue God's vision, though, is that it is His vision that brings Him the greatest delight. Our grandest ideas pale in comparison to His plans for us. And, if we are truly in tune with Him, then doing whatever brings honor, glory and pleasure to God is what makes our life worth living.

Often, human vision is dangerous because it is ego-driven. Instead, when we strive to understand and pursue God's vision, we exhibit a satisfying degree of obedience, submission and humility. Our vision may be something to which we could commit; but His vision is something over which we should obsess.

Do not reject a vision because it isn't what you were hoping for. If it is truly God's vision, it is perfect and He will bless you as you seek to fulfill it. Do not assume it is not His vision for you simply because it is uncomfortable. Whenever you devote yourself to obeying God, you declare yourself an enemy of Satan and of the world – and you'd better expect opposition and suffering. Great Christian leaders enter the battlefield aware of the challenge they have lodged, prepared to fight the good fight rather than to seek the easy path. Just as the apostle Paul had to suffer many things for the sake of Christ, the more responsible a soldier we become in the Lord's army, the weightier the challenges that we can expect to face. Faith in God and continued joy in being able to serve Him as a leader will move us beyond anything we might have otherwise achieved in life.

Maximizing the Vision

To make the most of the vision that God reveals to you, protect it and convey it to those who will partner with you in pursuing it.

Initially, thank God for allowing you to receive the vision and for the incredible responsibility and trust He has extended to you as the leader who has been given such vision. It is His gift to you – a tool to facilitate effective leadership, significant ministry and life meaning and transformation for many. Own that vision as dearly as anything in your life, being both humbled and energized by it. Pray constantly that He will bless you as you pursue it, and never fail to give Him the glory as aspects of the vision become reality. Commit yourself to faithfully and endlessly carry out that challenge.

In the process, remember that you are now the champion of the vision. You must protect it from being dissipated, ignored and half-heartedly carried out. One of your key roles, then, is to spread the vision. You must use whatever means are at your disposal to communicate the vision to those who will play a part in its life. That demands that you write the vision in a comprehensive fashion – an exhaustive documentation of the vision, as you understand it, in its totality. Also write a vision statement – a brief summary of the heart of the vision, captured in 15 to 25 words that are descriptive, precise, and inspiring, identifying the action that is required. Raise the vision during meetings and discussions, and relate decisions back to the vision. Evaluate outcomes in light of the vision. Hire staff in relation to their acceptance and passion regarding the vision of the ministry unit with which they will most commonly interface. Never let people forget the vision; that is a leader's task.

Keeping the vision alive is critical, but striving to strategically accomplish the vision is the bottom line for church leaders. Unless you act on it, vision is just a dream – interesting, but ultimately worthless. The failure to implement the vision is a rejection of God's gift to you and His plan for His people. Faithfully executing strategies and tactics that make His vision real will bring purpose, joy and influence into your life and that of the church.

Team Vision
Versus Church Vision

Now let's clarify the relationship between the vision of the church, the team and the individual leader.

From a leadership vantage point, the church operates at two levels: the aggregate, congregational level and the component ministry level. The aggregate level encompasses everything the church does. It is a core obligation of the Senior Pastor, as the primary, God-ordained leader of the church, to identify and articulate that corporate vision for the congregation. The pastor must not simply impose his/her vision for the church on the congregation, but must listen to God and discern what He has in mind for the church. The pastor then communicates God's vision for comprehensive ministry of the church to the body of members. Everything that takes place at the church from that point forward must be filtered through the simple question: Does this proposed activity or policy support our vision? In essence, this church vision statement is an umbrella vision, all activity within the church must be considered in light of the church's vision, no matter what the component ministry focus might be.

The pastor, alone, cannot make the vision happen; he/she will work with a team of leaders at the corporate level to ensure that the church stays on target. That corporate-level leadership team, perhaps comprised of the Senior Pastor and a handful of elders or other key lay leaders, is responsible for making sure that the vision is known, understood, owned and pursued by the congregation.

At the same time, that vision will become real through the work of various component ministries within the church, such as worship, evangelism, discipleship, stewardship, community service, and congregational community. In other words, the corporate vision is made real through teams of leaders whose efforts are blessed by the corporate leadership team in order to orchestrate the church's ministry development and vision fulfillment. Each of the component ministries will identify its own vision statement for its area of focus. Its vision will fit within the church's. By pursuing its own purpose, it will be facilitating the achievement of the church's, macro-level vision. Each component ministry will pursue its vision by developing goals, strategies and tactics related to its arena of ministry activity, designed to facilitate the ministry and spiritual maturing of congregants. Consequently, each component ministry will have its own team to articulate its vision, develop its plans, lead work groups and ancillary teams in carrying out its vision, and interact with the corporate leadership team to coordinate all ministry efforts.

When a ministry team strives to determine its vision, it will have two primary constraints. First, its team vision must fit snuggly within the contours and confines of the church's aggregate ministry. Second, the team's ministry will result from a combining of the personal visions of the team members – individuals who share a common passion for involvement in, and leadership of, that component of ministry. These individuals bring their visions to the team for consideration of what God wants to do among them.

The Saga of First Baptist Church

Here is an example of how the process works. James Barton was called as pastor of First Baptist eleven years ago.[4] Located in the Midwest, the church owned its small but tidy facility in a valley of mixed industrial and agricultural businesses, populated mostly by middle class and blue collar families. The church had about 300 adults attending on a regular basis, plus 80-some children and teens who participated in the youth program. Upon arriving, it became clear to him that there was a lot of ministry activity, but the efforts were not related to a grand vision of what God wanted First Baptist to accomplish in light of the kingdom. The church was simply doing its best to do what churches do – provide a worship service and Christian education program every Sunday, a family service Sunday night, a youth program on Wednesdays, and a parcel of other ministries (women's, men's, soup kitchen, etc.) whenever those groups were able to do something.

Pastor Barton spent about four months getting to know the people at First Baptist, and becoming familiar with the other ministers and churches in town. He spent time gathering facts about the community and its population, as well as delving into the history of First Baptist. After this period of "doing my homework," Pastor Barton began meeting with key congregants to ask for their support in what he described as the most important chapter in the church's 70-year history: seeking God's vision for the church. He was able to enlist several dozen leaders and other church members in praying for him and with him, and preparing themselves for a new era in the church's life.

Another seven months went by before Pastor Barton felt that he had truly heard from God regarding why He wanted First Baptist to continue, and how it could benefit the kingdom. The pastor spent another month carefully describing the outlines of vision to key leaders and church members, seeking their input and reshaping the vision around their ideas. The heart of the vision did not change, but the ways in which he began to convey the vision reflected some of the insights, experiences, passions and sensitivities of his congregants. Eventually, after minor revisions to the church values statement, the pastor crafted the following mission and vision statements:

Mission statement:

To love God and His creation through a biblical ministry of worship, discipleship, evangelism, and service.

Vision statement:

To promote constant and genuine worship, in multiple forms and venues, throughout the Valley, to strengthen believers and transform non-believers.

Pastor Barton spent the next quarter attempting to break down the vision into a palatable perspective for everyone who called First Baptist their church home. His deliberations had persuaded him that God was calling First Baptist, which had an outstanding worship ministry and a glut of capable musicians, to become the premiere worship ministry in the area. More importantly, though, Barton was struck by the notion that worship was to be the church's means of impacting people's lives – fortifying the spiritual strength of congregants through a deep and intense experience with God and His Word, as well as exposing non-believers to the presence of God through worship. The vision called for the church to base all of its ministry endeavors, both on and off the church's modest campus, on riveting worship. That meant offering to provide worship segments at local conferences, at public meetings, to help other churches with their worship ministries, and so forth. This was a big step for First Baptist: it had never been known for its worship, but now its primary thrust would be to focus on how authentic, intense worship could transform saints and sinners alike.

To get this vision across to people in the congregation, the pastor spent that three month period preaching, teaching, meeting, speaking and writing articles for church publications regarding the meaning and implications of the vision statement. He had two or three one-to-one meetings almost four days each week for a month, meeting with the church's influencers to lay out in detail the implications of the vision for the church and for the individual with whom he was meeting. He also spent time interacting with area pastors, informing them of the new developments and initiating conversations as to how First Baptist might be able to minister more cooperatively with other churches.

Finally, after three months of such preparation, he gained the enthusiastic endorsement of the mission and vision statements by the existing lay leaders and then by the entire congregation.

His next task was to align the church's organizational structure with the vision and some of the initial goals he set for the church in response to the vision statement. Having come from a team-based ministry in his prior church, Pastor Barton was determined to transition First Baptist to a church led by lay teams. He conceived a transition process, complete with phases focused on communicating the concept, gaining individual and committee support, identifying a pilot team and lay leaders, inviting those leaders to participate in specific ministry leadership teams, providing sufficient leadership training, instituting an organizational transition process for the church, and releasing the teams to lead. That process, which had some serious conflicts when a group of long-term elders resisted being reassigned to different positions, took slightly more than two years to put into effect.

By the time the transition was completed, Pastor Barton was working smoothly with the Executive Ministry Team of First Baptist. That team consisted of the pastor, who was a Directing leader; two elders, one of whom was a Strategic leader and another who was an Operational leader; and an additional layman, who was a gifted Team-Building leader. (The church did not use those names for their leaders, although they were cognizant of the diverse leadership gifts and skills each brought to the process, and came to appreciate the synergistic results.) After overcoming the typical discomforts and struggles of a newly-formed team – e.g., not always accepting the ideas of the Pastor, striving to understand the perspective of colleagues who come from different emotional or intellectual starting points, interpreting the vision differently in relation to various opportunities or challenges – the team began to appreciate its diversity and breadth of capacity, and more readily debated topics passionately, took bolder risks with programs and events, and more easily trusted each other's judgments in sensitive areas of ministry.

As part of their organizational re-engineering plan, the Executive Ministry Team (EMT) instituted four lay leadership teams to direct four programmatic ministries in the church: worship, discipleship, evangelism, and service. Those four were chosen to coincide with the church's mission statement. After an exhausting process of seeking to identify true leaders within the church, sixteen people agreed to serve on the leadership teams – four per component ministry. Those leaders were placed within their component ministry team because of a deep passion that each held for that ministry component. The EMT then charged each team with developing its own vision, which would coincide with that of the church at-large. After several months of concerted effort, each team enthusiastically produced its vision statement for feedback from the EMT. The vision statements of each team were as follows:

Worship Ministry Vision:
To incorporate a genuine worship experience into every public event at the church, and to offer other churches and organizations in the area access to our worship capabilities and resources.

Discipleship Ministry Vision:
To provide systematic biblical instruction in the context of a meaningful connection with God through teaching, song and prayer at every church activity.

Evangelism Ministry Vision:
To positively influence the lives of non-Christians through worship that provides the presence of God, through significant

relationships with worshiping parishioners, and through tailored teaching that demonstrates the relevance of God to non-Christians' lives.

Service Ministry Vision:

To reflect God's love and concern through the regular delivery of tangible resources to the needy of the Valley, as well as personal invitations to worship God with our church family.

Although Pastor Barton was concerned that those statements tended to be a bit wordy, he was visibly moved that each team had so clearly caught the thrust of the church's vision and had so passionately incorporated the worship emphasis into every component ministry. He let the component vision statements stand as they were, with the plan to make them more manageable once each team was immersed in carrying them out. He did not want to discourage them right away by suggesting that their vision was inappropriate. He sensed the heartbeat of each, and chose to work with statements whose verbosity was overshadowed by their intensity and intentionality.

Meanwhile, the church's elder board was redefined as a smaller group of godly individuals whose primary responsibility would be to keep the church accountable to its vision and to scriptural principles. The elders were to remain in contact with each leadership team and to serve as spiritual mentors to the church's leaders, while also examining the goals, strategies and tactics of each team to ensure that they reflected biblical integrity. The elders thus transitioned from being a policy-making group – that function was now handled by the EMT and the component ministry teams – to a direct ministry group, overseeing prayer, spiritual purity and congregational care within the church.

As the church settled into this new life, it found that additional lay leaders emerged, some rising from within the congregation and some being attracted to the church from the outside. Because the primary component teams had the leaders they needed, the first offer made to new leaders was to serve as apprentices to the existing leaders.

After their apprenticeships had been completed, those individuals were then invited to initiate new ministry teams that operated alongside the existing ministry team. For instance, the first new leadership team was a worship team that focused on facilitating worship among the young people in the congregation. The next team added was one that took on responsibility for service ministries to individuals who were immobile (e.g., prison inmates, shut-ins).

As the leadership capacity of the church grew, so did its attendance and budget, but not its staff. The associate who had been on the payroll when Barton arrived remained for a couple of years, until the transition to team-based ministry was completed, before leaving for another church. The church did hire a new associate, whose primary duties related to assisting the lay teams that directed the four component ministries. Pastor Barton, meanwhile, reported that he was enjoying ministry more than he had at any prior time in his life – a sentiment echoed by many of his congregants, and by nearly all of the church's lay leaders.

"It has been an interesting odyssey," he reflected. "I give all the credit to the people in this church, who were able to envision what could happen if we took the risk of changing the structure and our entire approach to leadership. We're just an average congregation, I suppose, but we have tremendous team leaders at work here. Their commitment, their gifts, their mutual respect and trust – it has really been a blessing to watch them take the concept and run with it. And it all began with their acceptance of God's vision for us – an enthusiastic, energetic adoption of that simple, 18-word statement that has allowed us to add a strategic piece to the ministry puzzle here in the Valley."

FOOTNOTES

[1] A national survey we conducted among a random sample of 602 Senior Pastors of Protestant churches revealed that less than one out of every twenty pastors was able to identify God's vision for the church's ministry. A concurrent survey conducted among a national sample of more than 400 born again Christians showed that an even smaller proportion of

believers was able to articulate God's vision for their life and ministry.

[2] I have written much more extensively on mission, vision and values in previous books. For greater detail on vision in ministry, consult *Turning Vision Into Action* (Ventura, CA: Regal Books, 1994); *The Power of Vision* (Ventura, CA: Regal Books, 1991); and chapter three of *Leaders On Leadership* (Ventura, CA: Regal Books, 1997).

[3] Additional discussion of the relationship of these elements to each other and to ministry is provided in my previous book, *Church Marketing: Breaking Ground for the Harvest* (Ventura, CA: Regal Books, 1992).

[4] The names have been changed to protect the church's privacy.

CHAPTER FOUR

WHY TEAMS ARE SCARCE
AND WHY THEY SHOULDN'T BE

Churches are among the most predictable subjects on which a researcher could focus. They change slowly, when they change at all, and churches are famous for creating and retaining traditions for long periods of time. Without wanting to be pejorative or discouraging, it is safe to predict that most Protestant churches will not incorporate team leadership into their ministry practices in the foreseeable future. In spite of the abundance of compelling reasons to do so, most churches will persist in emphasizing solo leadership. Let's figure out why.

Ten Reasons **Not** to Use Teams

Our research discovered more than a dozen common reasons why churches either refuse to use leadership teams, or have otherwise remained ignorant of the value of team-based leadership. Here's a brief description of some of the most common reasons.

Simplicity

Have you ever tried working in a team environment? If you have, then you know first-hand that if you compare leading as a team with leading by yourself, it's sometimes easier to lead without the encumbrance of other people, even if they generally believe the same things and desire the same ends as you. Over the course of time, as a team gels, the process may become smoother, easier and even faster than the experience of leading without a team. A variety of research studies show that mature teams typically produce far superior results to what a solo leader is able to achieve. But there is no denying that, at least in the early life stage of a team, it may be easier to lead solo than within a team.

Why is this true? In a team, everyone must be on the same page if the job is to be done effectively and efficiently. That requires meetings, discussion, and persuasion – in other words, it is an effort that demands more time, more energy and more resources to reach the same outcome that the individual leader may already embrace.

The other common obstacle that we encountered in this regard is the feeling among many leaders that they do a better job than anyone else might, even if others understand the situation, have useful skills and want to help. "Look, whenever I get other people involved, yes, there's wider ownership of the process, but the results are just not as good as what I can produce working on my own," explained one pastor with whom we spoke about team leadership. "I can get it done faster, cheaper, smarter, and better. That's not my ego, that's just the truth. People appreciate my ability to get the job done efficiently. That's why they hired me. There are other ways they can use their abilities to serve the church."

The chances are good that such a church will never reach its true ministry potential as long as such a person is the primary leader of the ministry. The church will be limited by that person's capacity to produce results. Such a pastor becomes both a production bottleneck as well as a person who sends a harmful message to the congregation: nobody is as good as the pastor, nor can they hope to become as productive. That message has a daunting effect on people's willingness to pull their weight in the church.

Control

If your church uses teams to propel the church forward, it has decentralized the ministry. That is a difficult thing for many churches to accomplish. Often, the overwhelming tendency is to maintain tight control over the procedures of the church. Giving up control is a major issue for many individuals and remains a major obstacle for tens of thousands of American churches.

Often, when a church or program is led by someone who is not truly a leader or by someone who lacks self-confidence or experience, the natural tendency is to dictate what must be done, rather than to rely upon the wisdom and breadth of experience resident within a group of leaders. The result is that creativity is stifled and decisions are limited by the intelligence, sensitivity and experience of the dictator. Naturally, people are less likely to feel ownership of the choices made for them than if there had been a more inclusive process at work.

Trying to serve within an environment in which one individual is controlling and domineering becomes oppressive. People lose interest, ministry becomes a labor rather than a joy, and results do not reach the heights that might have been achieved within a more inviting process. Usually, however, the controlling leader cannot see that reality and dismisses such "complaints" as the narrow-minded, unenlightened views of those who are jealous, power-hungry or immature.

Personal Significance

Whether due to fragile egos or misperception, many leaders eschew the team approach because it reduces the perceived value of the individual. If the team is making decisions and providing leadership, then the individual is no longer the center of attention, thereby minimizing his/her perceived importance to the ministry. Many leaders fight hard to maintain complete authority because they have a deep-seated need to be needed. Whether they feel that they are indispensable or have a need to feel so depends upon the person – but the outcome is the same, regardless of the driving motivation.

The bottom line is that the introduction of team-based leadership is a personal threat to such an individual. Rather than focusing upon the good of the ministry, these people look only to what's best for themselves and would rather experience personal status and prestige than to do what is right for the ministry.

Efficiency

How often have you heard someone dismiss the idea of working with others by lightly noting, "I can do it faster by myself?" This is sometimes accurate. After all, a team may require meetings to identify the challenges and tasks, information gathering, planning, discussion of the options, resolution of resulting conflict and confusion – in other words, it is likely that more time and energy will be consumed in getting to a point of decision and implementation.

Accepting such an argument, however, assumes that the only significant outcome is to do something, regardless of the quality of the action and its product. Only in exceptional instances is it likely that the results of one person will outweigh the results of a competent team of individuals working together toward a common goal. Achieving the fastest turnaround does not always produce "excellence" in the product.

Tradition

For the last quarter-century it has become common practice to criticize churches for not trying new things, or not doing things in a new way. In spite of the widespread ridicule of stubborn adherence to outdated tradition and practices, though, thousands of churches continue to resist reasonable change. It has been said that the seven last words of the Church will be "we've never done it that way before."

Using teams as the means of leadership is outside the traditional boundaries of most churches. One pastor clearly expressed his views on this during my conversation with him: "You know, we've been providing godly leadership for our people for seven decades without using this team concept, and we'll probably continue to provide godly leadership for another seven decades without introducing team leadership." The fact that his church had not experienced an increase in attendance or budget in the past decade, that there was an average of less than two conversions per year at his church, or that few people spent any time outside of the church services relating to Christ and studying God's Word apparently was irrelevant in his mind. His church was comfortable with its routine and was not concerned about the results. After all, they were doing what their church had always done. Introducing a team-based leadership approach might be interpreted by some as saying that the church's founders and predecessors had not lived up to their potential.

Don't Know How

Another common argument offered by many churches against using teams is that they have never been trained to work as team leaders and therefore cannot make the transition away from solo leadership. Although there are team leadership books, videotapes, conferences, seminars, and other training resources widely accessible, few pastors and church staff people have been exposed to such training. (Interestingly, we discovered that many lay leaders have used such resources as part of their vocational training.) The issue is not really that church leaders cannot get the training they need to create a viable team process, but that it is not a priority for them.

Once again, it seems that the excuse that is given masks a deeper reservation – namely, that the individual does not truly embrace the team approach. Given the availability of resources that would facilitate a workable move toward team leadership, not knowing how to make the change is a weak excuse – but one that we found many pastors offer as a daunting obstacle.

Nobody Models It

Some church leaders noted that they do not work within leadership teams because they have not seen it modeled for them in other churches. This concern generally means that either team leadership is not sufficiently widespread to qualify, in their eyes, as a practice worth replicating, or that there is not an example of team leadership that they could learn from. Either way, this excuse highlights one of the unfortunate diseases that characterize many churches: ministry by mimicry.

Over the past ten years we have found that when an organization lacks strong leadership, the tendency is to find a competing or similar organization that is successful and to copy whatever that group seems to be doing. This strategy rarely works for the imitator because it does not understand the underlying structure and the different context within which the successful entity operates. Further, the imitator typically tries to implement its facsimile of the original model in a very compressed period of time, effectively precluding the church from truly grasping the foundational ministry philosophy that allowed the process to work in the church where it originated.

The idea that team leadership has not been witnessed in other ministries raises two concerns. The first is that most church leaders do not actually get to scrutinize the operations and ministry activity of other churches. The typical pastor or staff person attends an average of one or two seminars and conferences per year. Often, those are events sponsored by very large churches of national reputation (e.g., Willow Creek Community Church, Saddleback Community Church, First Assembly of Phoenix), which means that their exposure to ministry is limited to a few wonderful but atypical churches. Second, the absence of exposure to team leadership reminds us that there are not enough churches engaging in this practice to make it a visible and noticeable element in almost any church whose ministry is being observed or studied.

Vision

Leadership teams serve within the boundaries of the macro-level vision cast by the primary leaders of the organization. One of the barriers to using teams, then, is the absence of vision within the church. A survey we conducted several years ago showed that very few pastors (less than one in ten) were able to articulate God's vision for their church. The consequence is that the church is not really going anywhere special, unique or significant: it is simply a ministry outpost doing good works, but without an understanding of its unique and necessary role within the kingdom.

Naturally, if the church at-large does not have a clear and compelling sense of God's vision, then the leaders within the church will lack such purpose and direction as well. If the church tried to fashion a team-based leadership process, to where would those teams lead the church? Without clear vision, they have no destination. The only real objective would be to help the church survive, which is the antithesis of godly leadership. His leaders exist to facilitate spiritual transformation and maturity; encouraging believers and a congregation to accept a spiritual holding pattern requires no leadership.

The Pastor's Role

In a team environment, the leadership role of the pastor shifts from that of leading the entire congregation to being a leader of leaders. This is exactly the role that Jesus exemplified: rather than shepherd the thousands, He shepherded the twelve, who then led the throngs who were attracted to the Lord. This reduces the stress on the pastor from having to be all things to all people – and, essentially, becoming nothing to everyone. He/she may instead pour whatever they have to offer into the relative handful of fellow leaders, who in turn will provide the breadth and depth of leadership that the church requires.

For thousands of pastors, we have seen that this transition is improbable. They were raised to believe that the pastor leads everyone and must have direct, unfettered oversight in the lives of the masses. The problem is that if one clings to that perspective, the leader will never have the chance to lead masses in the first place because people who are serious about spiritual growth simply will not put up with what amounts to superficial leadership.

Perhaps we can adapt an old axiom and posit that it takes a mature person to embrace team leadership, because it demands giving up the spotlight, authority and the view of the pastor as the center of all church activity.

Church Culture

As will be discussed later in this book, making the move to teams will fail unless the transition happens within the context of a church culture that demands and esteems teamwork. You cannot simply accept the idea of team leadership and try to implement it within an operational structure that is not designed to facilitate teams, or a culture that does not resonate with teamwork.

Your church has a culture – every organization has an operating culture. That culture is comprised of all of the symbols, traditions, assumptions, customs, ideals, values, language and systems that interpret and deliver your ministry reality. Culture is what gives context and meaning to your experience. That culture is continually evolving, but once its foundation has been laid, it takes extraordinary effort and intentionality to modify it.

Most churches would rather live within the confines of an unhealthy culture than to go through the painstaking transformation that a cultural shift would require. If your church has always used solo leadership, becoming a team-led church would demand a complete re-thinking of many core values and practices such as defining the role of the pastor, delegating responsibility and authority, establishing accountability, developing true community, determining priorities and goals, and creating a viable organizational structure.

We Can Do Better

Do any of those ten justifications for avoiding team leadership reign within your church? If so, please think and pray about the implications of refusing to use a process that has so often proven to be more effective than its alternatives.

Indisputably, shifting from solo leadership to team leadership is a major transition, and will bring with it all of the challenges common to making any significant change in behavior and philosophy. The churches that have blazed the trail before you, though, unanimously indicated to us that the hard work was well worth the effort.

Few ministry philosophies I have studied come as highly recommended as leading through teams. "I can tell you all the benefits we have experienced from switching to teams," explained the senior pastor of one of the churches we studied that transitioned to teams. "At the time we changed over [from solo leadership] I remember that I had some doubts about it being a smart thing to do. It didn't happen overnight and the transition wasn't without its moments of frustration and disappointment. But to be honest, I can't remember a single one of those doubts today. That probably speaks volumes to the fact that the advantages have been so overwhelming that I can't even recall what my concerns were. This transition has been a total win-win situation for us."

At the start of this chapter, I mentioned that I would identify some compelling reasons to incorporate a team leadership approach. Hopefully, you can already sense that the dominant objections and obstacles to team leadership are indefensible excuses. To strengthen the argument in favor of team leadership – and, perhaps, your resolve to move toward a team-based ministry – let me describe ten benefits of using team leadership in your ministry.

1. The Bible Endorses It

Our ministry principles and methods should be derived from the Bible. In studying the lives of God's chosen leaders portrayed in Scripture, we find a variety of models. Jesus devoted His years of public ministry to developing a team of leaders who then led the early Church after His death and resurrection. Paul was a devoted team practitioner, traveling with various teams. Moses led in tandem with Joshua and Aaron by his side. David and Nehemiah may be included among the other leaders who worked with teams.

The Bible does not provide us with a direct admonition to provide team-based leadership, but it does teach the value of community, unity, diversity, mutual trust, and the interrelationship of gifts – all aspects that lead to a team-based approach. Looking at the issue from a different angle, the Word clearly teaches that we are not to be independent of God, nor to be overly self-confident or to strive to accomplish things in our own strength and power. Again, such a perspective moves us closer to embracing a team-oriented strategy for growing the Church, because it teaches us to look outward, not inward.

2. No More Superheroes

The often-heard complaint – there just aren't enough lay leaders to make the church's ministry happen – is not an accurate representation of the situation. What we lack are the dynamic, high-energy, driven, charismatic, compelling leaders who have become the icons of our culture – individuals ranging from Jack Welch, Ronald Reagan, Lee Iacocca to Steve Jobs and Peter Ueberroth. In the church world we elevate extraordinary leaders such as Bill Hybels, Rick Warren, Kirbyjon Caldwell, Paul Cho, Jack Hayford and Ted Haggard to that same level of leadership "super stardom." But most people do not have the mix of gifts, talent, experience and opportunity that has enabled these individuals to gain notoriety.

The fact that few people possess such incredible leadership capacity is an important realization. It means that most churches are resigned to one of two outcomes: consistent failure due to the lack of available high-impact leaders, or reliance upon a different leadership paradigm. Given our understanding that God takes pleasure in His people succeeding, that He never sets up His followers for failure, and that the Church is God's instrument for ministry throughout the world, we can confidently assert that He has provided us with all the leaders we need to accomplish the aims of the Church. Therefore, we ought to recognize that the prevailing idea about leadership – namely, that people are to be led by the powerhouse individual leaders – is simply wrong.

Once we embrace the idea that leadership can be capably – and often, even more capably – done by teams, then we can shed our inferiority complexes and stop looking for the hidden superheroes. Instead, we must help every believer to identify his/her gifts and abilities, and release those with the gift of leadership to serve people through that God-given capacity. As management pioneer Peter Drucker sagely observed, "The purpose of a team is to make the strengths of each person effective and his or her weaknesses irrelevant."[1]

3. True Community

A hallmark of an authentic Christian church is that its people are not merely acquaintances who share a sanctuary once a week, but that they are a community of people who believe the same things, follow the same Lord, and love each other. Since the congregation often takes its cues from the church's leaders, it is important that the leaders be united, mutually trusting and supportive, and serving in harmony. There is no better way to foster such leadership than in a team environment.

One of the beautiful outcomes of lay leadership that occurs within teams is that the congregation quickly understands that ministry is done by the laity and that the church exemplifies cooperation in its performance of its duties. That is a key message for the congregation to absorb: we are one in vision, in relationship and in ministry, as modeled by the church leaders.

4. Less Stress

If we can reduce the burden of leadership shouldered by church leaders, one outcome would be a reduction in the stress levels they feel. While Scripture alludes to the hardships of ministry, it does not suggest that we must add to the pressures of living a holy and servant-based life by placing incredible – sometimes unreasonable – expectations upon mere mortals. One viable means of reducing stress levels is by working in teams.

Leadership, by its very nature, will produce stress. Whenever you seek to motivate people to change the way they think or live, stress will emerge. Whenever you make decisions that affect people's lives, you will experience the stress of responsibility. Whenever you battle the forces of evil for the glory of God, stress will be a by-product of the battle. Stress is an unavoidable hazard that leaders cope with from the time they begin leading until they retire from such service. In fact, one of the characteristics of effective leaders is that they can handle the stress and pressure that they encounter as they fulfill their leadership obligations.

Team-oriented leadership does not eliminate stress, but it does reduce it by sparing the individual from having to be the expert in everything. The workload is shared, the decision-making is carried out in cooperation with other skilled and insightful partners, and the gifts required to do an excellent job are resident within the team. The anxiety that comes from recognizing that you are in over your head may not be completely eliminated. After all, God's desire is that we rely upon Him for our strength and direction, so if it became too easy we'd become independent and arrogant. Team leaders can serve with greater assurance and serenity because of the strength of the team.

5. Greater Synergy

"One of the lessons I finally absorbed is that a team always outperforms an individual, no matter how gifted that individual may be," declared one pastor we interviewed. "I used to pride myself on my ability to get things done and to get people excited about what I'd done, but eventually I burned out and realized that if I had simply opened my eyes, recognized the warehouse of talent the Lord brought here, and allowed other people to use their abilities, we'd all be better off. Our teams don't just increase the impact of the leaders, they multiple them several times over."

A true team generates results far greater than the sum of the parts could have achieved. One of the ways that you can tell if a team is firing on all cylinders is by evaluating their output: if it substantially exceeds what would have occurred had the team members been leading on a solo basis, then the team is functional. If the team is merely producing results equal to what they would have produced if each individual were working independently, then the team is not at its optimal level. (There are various reasons for that shortfall – inappropriate matching of aptitudes, an inferior captain, an ambiguous process – all of which will be discussed later.)

One of the great joys of team leadership is participating in a synergistic process. "It's like a bonus," exclaimed one of the lay leaders to whom we spoke. "After a while, you just enjoy working with these other people so much that you can't imagine leading any other way, but then when you see the results shoot off the chart, well, you start to realize that the combined efforts of properly matched leaders can produce unimaginable results."

6. More Innovation

Leaders solve problems. Great leaders solve problems creatively, enabling them to overcome a broader range of problems and to devise lasting solutions to vexing challenges. Imagine what happens when you team a group of creative problem solvers who embrace the same vision. The result is a plethora of new ideas, a higher level of innovative thinking, and a heightened willingness to take reasonable risks that may launch the ministry to another level of impact.

As our culture becomes more complicated and people's attention and energy is diverted from the things of God, we will need more creative responses to engage people in spiritual development and ministry. A great idea is a great idea, whether it comes from one person or a team. But the evidence indicates that the push-and-pull dynamic that occurs among a group of individuals with a shared commitment and true leadership capacity is likely to outdistance anything that the lone-ranger leader conceives.

7. Greater Joy

People love to succeed. Leadership, being the challenging calling that it is, provides its practitioners with an emotional and spiritual high when they experience victories en route to their ultimate destination.

Leading as a team, though, produces a superior sense of joy. Why? Just as a parent experiences more profound joy when something wonderful happens to the family than when in reaction to a personal achievement, so does a team leader feel greater joy when the team facilitates a positive outcome. In other words, participation in a team process often becomes a reward in itself through the distinctive experiences that emerge from the group process and relationships.

Not surprisingly, we also found that the results derived through team efforts may exceed those that would have been achieved through individual effort, further increasing the satisfaction through teamwork.

8. The Priesthood of Believers

Team-based leadership is surely an extension of the Ephesians 4 exhortation for us to equip the saints for ministry, in the same way that Peter and John discussed the importance of believers forming a priesthood of believers who serve together.[2] God has entrusted a wealth of resources to His people – spiritual gifts, money, time, relationships, material possessions, opportunities, ideas, information – for the purpose of knowing, loving and serving Him. In fact, team-oriented ministry is one of the means of deploying the gifts that people possess for maximum ministry potential. But just as Paul wrote that no person has all of the spiritual gifts given by God, neither does any individual have all the attributes necessary to lead with perfection. It is through mutual reliance that leaders achieve their highest potential.

9. Facilitates Numerical Growth

Churches that exhibit great leadership grow because the people that attend those churches understand the vision of the church; are motivated to participate in the fulfillment of that vision; are encouraged to use their unique gifts and abilities to contribute to the church's ministry; are teamed with others whose gifts and skills complement their own; and are encouraged to develop the resources required to have the desired impact. People are attracted to strong visionary leadership. Churches that provide such direction and support are magnetic, invariably growing both numerically as well as spiritually.

Unfortunately, many large churches lose their spiritual edge because their leaders fail to deputize lay leaders to push the church to its potential. The dynamic teaching or charismatic personality of a pastor can only take a church so far. Such individuals may attract large numbers of people, but unless they provide true leadership, which facilitates spiritual transformation, the church will simply become a religious event center with increasingly demanding observers. When congregants who have been called by God to lead are brought together in teams, and given the responsibility and authority to lead, the ministry becomes decentralized and is thus capable of increased growth – numerical and spiritual.

10. Relieves the Senior Pastor

Most churches remain wholly dependent upon the abilities and energy of their pastor. When teams take over the leadership load, the pastor is freed to deliver what he/she has uniquely been called and gifted to bring to the church. In team-led churches we discovered that pastors enjoy their vocation more, they stay at their church longer, they are less prone to burnout, and the church is healthier spiritually.

Teams Make Sense

Can you understand why every church we interviewed that has gone the team leadership route raves about the impact? It makes sense, but it also has a proven track record in practice. Developing a workable team process is neither quick nor easy, but with the right level of commitment and resources, the transition is likely to be well worth the effort.

But what does it take to pull this off successfully? Our study showed that developing great team leadership is a matter of how you work with your people, the process you implement and sustain, and the product that you seek. Let's explore the experience of churches that have done this successfully.

FOOTNOTES

[1] Peter Drucker, *Managing the Non-Profit Organization*; New York: HarperCollins, 1990, pages 122-125.
[2] Peter writes of the priesthood of believers in 1 Peter 2:5-6. John addresses this in Revelation 1:5-6, 5:9-10, and 20:6.

CHAPTER FIVE

THE PEOPLE FACTOR IN TEAM DEVELOPMENT

Your church might have the best facilities in town, the greatest opportunities for impact and the most efficient systems in place, but without the right people, none of those conditions make much difference.

"It took me years to realize that although I understood the process of leadership development, I didn't have much understanding of who the right people were to invite into leadership," confessed one veteran Presbyterian pastor serving in Michigan. "Once I focused on getting the right people involved, everything started to click."

As you identify people for involvement in leadership teams at your church, you will save yourself and your church much stress and turmoil if you know what you're looking for from the start. You are seeking *leaders*, which means individuals who have been called by God to lead, who have godly character and who possess the competencies to help people fulfill God's vision for the group. In addition, you are also seeking to combine people of compatible leadership aptitudes and who have the ability to work effectively in a team setting.

Let's examine each of these areas more closely.

Calling

Every Christian is called by God to serve Him in a unique fashion, exploiting the gifts, talents, abilities, experiences, passions and opportunities He has provided to you. Each of us often serves God in ways that are outside of our area of calling – and He uses those efforts to the glory of His name and the benefit of His people. Our highest calling, of course, is to be disciples, doing whatever it takes to live according to His will for His followers. But He has also prepared us for special works that build upon intentional behavior that reflects the fruit of the Spirit (Gal. 5:22-24) or consistency with His commandments. When we take advantage of opportunities to serve Him within our area of calling we provide a unique, desirable and valued addition to His kingdom. The servant experiences a heightened degree of satisfaction in ministry, and those who are the recipients of such ministry also derive true benefit from the experience.

God calls every Christian to a role of service, but not everyone is called to be a leader (1 Corinthians 12:12-27). In fact, most people we read about in the Bible were not leaders, yet they served important roles within the development of God's kingdom. He calls each believer to fill a special role in His work, and corporately we fill a variety of roles within His kingdom. Each of those roles must be adequately fulfilled for His Church to realize its fullness.

The tension, of course, is that some people aspire to leadership even though God has neither called nor gifted them for such a position within His service. Churches often ignore the obvious mismatch between Godly calling and human desire, resulting in an awkward and sometimes harmful disparity of role and servant. Clearly and accurately knowing the nature of your calling is crucial; having an unshakeable certainty will motive you to persist in the face of resistance and challenges. Such conviction is especially important for those who believe they are called to lead. That particular calling is given to a select group of believers for the purpose of guiding God's people toward the fulfillment of the distinct vision He has given to them collectively, as well as the unique vision He provides to each believer individually. The call to lead is not superior to other roles to which people may be called, but the breadth of responsibility assigned to leaders demands that they be quite certain that God intends for them to serve in such a manner.

Calling is typically affirmed through several conditions. First, after extensive and intensive prayer, Bible study, and self-assessment, the individual senses God's calling to lead. When God calls a person to a task, it is imperative that they have conviction about it; without a deep passion for that work, the chances of having significant impact are limited, at best. Passion for the specific ministry calling enables a person to transcend the inevitable obstacles and difficulties related to accomplishing God's tasks.

Second, that call should be affirmed by those who know the individual well. If they do not endorse the calling as reasonable, further exploration is warranted. However, if the people who know the individual most intimately acknowledge the likelihood of his/her call to leadership, such support represents a strong endorsement. Throughout Scripture the individuals God called to be leaders were accepted by the people they were to lead, thereby strengthening the claim of such a calling.

Third, a called individual will possess the requisite spiritual gifts and leadership skills. Often, those gifts and skills need to be refined, but the presence of those resources in the individual is additional evidence of God's plan for the person. There is some contention as to which spiritual gifts a person should have in order to be an effective leader. Our research suggests that the gifts most likely to characterize a called leader are those within the group of "directive gifts," which enable a believer to direct the activities of individuals and groups within the body of Christ. The three Directive gifts are leadership, apostleship and pastoring. Individuals who have been granted these gifts generally provide comprehensive, vision-based direction to people that empowers and enhances their lives.

71

Fourth, the person's life experience reflects a tendency to serve as a leader, no matter what the circumstances might be. I have noticed over the years that a leader cannot help but lead; even when he/she is not in a leadership position, they cannot restrain their natural abilities of motivating, mobilizing, directing and resourcing people to pursue a compelling vision. When such leadership is not provided, it grates on them.

Recognizing a person's call to leadership is the starting point in the process of identifying who should be involved in leadership teams. If the call is not clear, work with the person to get a better sense of who God made them to be. Help the individual to go deeper in a self-discovery process to learn more about God's design for their life. But do not give them an assignment before you are confident that leadership is the role that God intends him/her to fill. Trying to convert non-leaders into leaders is a painful experience for the wanna-be leader as well as for those who will suffer through their misadventure.

Character

Human character reflects who we really are. The Bible is pretty clear that all of us are sinners and are crippled by the effects of sin. In spite of that handicap God uses His followers for His ends and chooses some to be leaders. A key to fulfilling that calling is to have a heart to become more like Christ. All believers are expected to possess such character, but it may become a more sensitive issue for Christian leaders because they become a role model to the world as well as the Church by virtue of their visibility and influence.

A worldly leader ascends the ladder of authority because of what he/she accomplishes. A godly leader is granted the privilege of leading God's people because of who they are – their heart to know, love and serve God by leading His people to fulfill His vision. As a result of that burning desire to serve in this way, and to honor God at all times by modeling righteousness and holy living, people are motivated to follow such a leader. Leadership becomes effective on the basis of character rather than salesmanship or style. In fact, leaders have their greatest influence on the basis of two special elements: the vision they convey and the character they possess. Without a compelling cause to support, a leader will generate little interest. Without attractive, godly character, a leader cannot generate confidence among the people.

Every great leader of God exhibits the brand of character attributed to David: "a man after my [God's] own heart" (Acts 13:22). The Bible clearly outlines the character traits that enable a person to be a Christian leader. While none of us is a perfect reflection of every one of those traits, we are to be generally consistent with, and to be constantly moving toward a more godly and righteous character. Harboring glaring character deficiencies or a stubborn refusal to submit to the Holy Spirit and the shaping influence of godly mentors to become a positive reflection of Christ disqualifies an individual from church leadership – no matter how skilled or talented that individual might be in leadership competencies. The kingdom of God is never so desperate for people who will participate in the work of the Church that biblical standards should be relaxed to accommodate a person of skills and high potential. God always cares more about who we are than about what we accomplish.

Perhaps the best recitation of the character qualities of Christian leaders is located in 1 Timothy 3. As you search for individuals who will provide excellent leadership within your church, examine the character of each individual to see how it measures up against the attributes Paul listed. You will never find a perfect match, but you will discover that God has brought your church many individuals who thirst for the holy lifestyle that Paul describes. If God is the potter, rest assured that there is good clay waiting to be molded into effective leaders for God.

Leadership Competencies

Competencies are the accumulation of skills, knowledge, experiences and abilities that allow a leader to lead. In a ministry context, competencies are the actions taken by leaders to intentionally and strategically facilitate positive life transformation that enables people to become more Christ-like. Competencies are the outgrowth of a Christian leader having a determination to serve God through leadership (calling), being in tune with God and thus knowing where to lead His people (vision), attracting followers through a demonstration of God's work in his/her life (character), and striving to provide people with the direction and tools they need to facilitate God-honoring change and growth.

For a leader to be effective, he/she must possess and utilize an array of competencies. Those skills combine to become the tools of the leader. The more tools the leader has, the more capacity he/she has to produce significant results. Unlike calling, competencies can be taught. Unlike character, the absence of particular competencies does not disqualify a God-ordained leader from serving the Church. You will find that most leaders within the Church have raw talent that needs to be recognized and refined. If the individual has been called by God to lead and both reflects and longs for Christ-like character, investing in that individual's development as a leader is worthwhile.

Since competencies are the actual efforts and abilities that leaders deploy to motivate, mobilize, resource and direct people toward fulfilling the vision God has provided for a group of believers, what are those competencies? There are several dozen that could be identified, but here is a brief description of fifteen leadership competencies that seem to be the most central tools in the toolbox of effective ministry leaders.

1. Identifying, articulating, casting God's vision.

The basic currency of leaders is vision. It is the light at the end of the tunnel to which every leader directs people, and it is the outcome that creates enthusiasm and hope in the minds and hearts of leaders and followers alike. Every leader must learn to identify God's unique vision for the ministry to which he/she has been called. Every leader must be able to persuasively share that vision with others, to motivate them to join in the effort to make the vision a reality. Every leader must exploit every opportunity to communicate that vision far and wide, to enlist people in the movement to bring God's ultimate plan to fruition. Remember: without vision at the center of one's leadership, there is nothing to lead people to – and, consequently, the individual is not truly a leader.

2. Coaching and developing other leaders.

While there is a difference between teachers and leaders, we have seen that leaders are always mentoring other leaders once they have absorbed enough skill and perspective to pass along to them. The notion of the master-apprentice relationship is usually evident in the lives of leaders: if they are not serving as an apprentice to a more skilled leader, then they are serving as a master leader tutoring those who wish to become more mature in their competencies. Great leaders recognize that their position and their ability is a gift from God to be shared with others for the common good. Effective leaders seek ways of delegating both responsibility and authority to those who are capable of handling those elements.

3. Developing and communicating strategies.

Communicating vision without also providing people with tangible ways of converting the vision into reality breeds frustration. Effective leaders must be able to break the vision into component pieces and develop strategies for implementing the vision. Those component pieces become discussion elements and assignments to be embraced by people who serve the church.

4. Motivating people to get involved.

A leader without followers is not really a leader. For the vision to become reality, people must become enthusiastic about the vision and the opportunity to fulfill God's plan. Leaders motivate people through God's vision, personal character and by providing people with realistic and doable tasks that bring the vision to pass. This implies the building of relationships, an effective communications process and a means of reinforcing people's participation in the cause.

5. Efficiently mobilizing ministry participants.

The energy and abilities of those who will cooperate in the pursuit of the vision must be efficiently orchestrated to facilitate the grand outcomes that leaders propose. Understanding people's gifts and abilities, recognizing their experience, and blending people into significant work teams is a key role of leaders. This entails the strategic allocation of resources, responsibility and power. But even more importantly, a great leader is one who is able to empower people to grow and to serve at their fullest capacity. Rallying people around a compelling vision and turning them loose, with direction, to pursue that vision is a critical dimension of leading people.

6. Resolving conflict.

Every team experiences conflict. Effective teams are prepared to handle the conflict and address the issues without allowing the related tensions to undermine the team or its efforts. Conflict resolution demands mutual trust, a level of commitment to the team's vision that transcends the importance of personal goals, a viable process for communication, and a heartfelt desire to maintain strong bonds within the group. The team must also be committed to acknowledging the existence of unhealthy tension and facing the situation before it festers.

7. Identifying, accumulating and utilizing resources appropriately.

No matter how enthusiastic the team may be, little can be accomplished without adequate resources. There are many types of resources: financial, human, spiritual, material, etc. Leaders must be able to recruit or acquire the resources needed to get the job done. In addition, a leader must be a good steward of the resources the Lord entrusts to them. The wise allocation of resources, efficient use of those elements and genuine gratitude for the availability of resources are central skills of an effective leader.

8. Reinforcing commitment and success.

God's vision is never easy to achieve. People will experience substantial challenges and even temporary defeats along the path to success, and such barriers may discourage them. Because we live in a busy society, and most Christians are trying to fit their faith into an already overwhelming schedule, individuals often become frustrated or fatigued. Leaders must be able to read the signs of discouragement, fatigue, and dissipating trust to keep people excited about the special role they play in the process. Similarly, when victories are achieved, it is important for leaders to supply appropriate reinforcement and celebration.

9. Objectively evaluating the ministry.

Progress demands an accurate sense of where you stand. Leaders must constantly know the pulse of the people and have a clear comprehension of what strategies do and do not work, as well as how much farther the ministry must go to achieve its ends. Leaders have a responsibility to protect people from failure whenever possible. But because leaders also have a responsibility to ensure that the ministry is operating at a level of excellence, some means of consistent evaluation of both quality and productivity is a key tool of an effective leader.

10. Intentionally shaping the corporate culture.

As noted in the previous chapter, every ministry develops an internal culture that greatly impacts it's ability to generate meaningful outcomes. Leaders must purposefully shape the culture of the ministry, integrating appropriate values, language, customs, systems, priorities, goals, and behavioral standards. The culture facilitates desired outcomes as well as provides parameters within which the ministry's adherents will live.

11. Modeling Christian character and commitment.

Because people learn by watching what other people whom they respect do, and leaders are usually among those from who the masses take their cues, it is imperative that the commitment to Christ and His vision for the ministry, as well as the Christian character of the leader, shine brightly. A true leader is not one who says "Do as I say, not as I do," but one who needs to say little because his/her actions speak for themselves. To lead in ministry, an individual should possess obvious spiritual maturity and genuine dedication to continually growing deeper in his/her faith. Great Christian leaders are authentically loving and caring people, and are not afraid to be "real" and vulnerable. Their integrity and humility must run deep.

12. Attracting and maintaining an effective team.

Leaders are always on the lookout for others who possess the same passion, gifting and calling that they have. Leaders love to be with other leaders. Providing fellow leaders an opportunity to contribute to the cause is a personal joy and a corporate benefit.

Once those individuals become part of the leadership family, maintaining healthy work and personal relationships remains a priority.

13. Leading by serving.

Perhaps the most profound leadership lesson that Jesus gave to His apprentices was that a leader is not the first among people, but the servant of all people. In a culture that fosters independence and personal achievement, perceiving and implementing leadership as a means of focusing on and addressing the needs of others is a foreign concept. Christian leaders must emulate the example of Jesus and pour themselves into building up and edifying the body of believers so that they, too, might devote themselves to selflessly serving others – that is, expressing the distinctive of a genuine, Christian love.

14. Solving problems and meeting challenges.

People turn to their leaders for direction, resources, strength and encouragement in the face of problems. A leader must have the capacity to study a situation, interpret the findings intelligently, conceive a strategic course of action, marshal the resources to implement the response, and to monitor the progress and make mid-course adjustments as necessary. In the same way, when non-problematic opportunities arise, a leader must know which of those opportunities to pursue and which to ignore.

15. Clarifying and promoting core values.

Defining what is worthy, important and appropriate – i.e., values – is a central function of an effective leader. Those values influence our culture, our character, our hopes for the future and our present-day behavior and morals. Internal consistency is a hallmark of effective leaders – but such consistency is not attainable unless a clear delineation of values is provided and upheld.

Let's be honest. Every leader does not shine with equal brightness in each of these dimensions. As we examine the concept of leadership aptitudes we will discover that every leader excels in some areas and performs merely adequately in others. Being able to recognize those relative strengths and weaknesses will become a critical element in developing effective teams.

Undoubtedly you can think of other important competencies that leaders must possess to help their church succeed. The fifteen attributes listed above are not meant to be an exhaustive list, but reflect what we have observed to be the most significant competencies in the lives of effective leaders. As you evaluate the people who might serve in a leadership capacity at your church, do they possess these competencies? If not, are they willing to develop them? Do they have the ability to grow in these areas?

Leadership Aptitudes

Just as public school teachers specialize in certain subjects that they teach, so do leaders have certain dimensions of leadership in which they are more proficient. The act of leading people and organizations covers a lot of ground. It is not reasonable to expect one individual to have all of the abilities, information, skills, gifts and experiences that would enable him/her to effectively lead. It is that very expectation, of course, that gets many churches into trouble, causing them to search for the superhero leader.

Every leader has what we have labeled a "dominant leadership aptitude," which refers to a specialization or emphasis within the leadership endeavor. A leadership aptitude is more than a style of leading; it incorporates a specific skill set, personality type and strategic perspective that moves the leader to emphasize one particular aspect of leadership more than the other aspects that comprise aggregate leadership.

Understanding leadership aptitudes and incorporating that knowledge into the development of the individual leader and into the blending and training of each team is crucial to success. Often, we found that churches arrive at this understanding through a painful combination of intuition and trial-and-error. Our study of leadership dynamics may help you shortcut the process without losing any of the outcomes.

There are four leadership aptitudes. Some leaders are best in the *directing* aspect of leadership. Others are best at the *strategic* development required for impact. Many leaders thrive on the *interpersonal* dimension of leadership and specialize in building networks and teams. Still others are at their best when they create *systems* that facilitate effective leadership and ministry. Because each of these approaches to leadership requires a different way of viewing reality, a different type of relationship with people, and a distinct set of skills within the leadership domain, it is not possible for any one individual to be the "complete" leader. In fact, if anyone possessed all four of these aptitudes, the best description of them would be "clinically schizophrenic." You would always be at war with yourself as your strove to see the world from disparate points of view, frustrated in developing relationships that serve leadership productivity, and overwhelmed by the breadth of output that must be delivered to move the ministry toward the fulfillment of its vision.

The upshot of this realization is that the ideal team is comprised of four leaders, each representing a different aptitude. In fact, we have seen time after time that the absence of any one of the four aptitudes renders the ministry vulnerable and unstable. A team that blends these four aptitudes is one that has the potential to accomplish great things for the kingdom, with excellence, efficacy and efficiency.

But what do these people look like? How do you know who represents each of these qualities? Here is a description of each of these types of leaders – their primary contribution to the team effort, their strengths and their weaknesses. They minister along-side of you every week. Do you recognize who these people are?

1. The DIRECTING Leader

Ronald Reagan was the quintessential directing leader. These are individuals who excel at conveying a compelling vision and who do not invest their energy in the details of the process. They motivate people to get involved or to feel encouraged by the appealing future they describe and the significant role that people may play in bringing that future to pass. These leaders rally people around the cause and get other leaders to understand and own the direction that they will jointly pursue to fulfill the vision.

Directing leaders are catalysts. They excite people's imaginations and enable them to believe in themselves. That motivational capacity attracts people to the cause. Directing leaders are effective public speakers and good listeners. They make people feel as if they matter.

Directing leaders are good decision-makers. They like to have the facts at their disposal, but as often as not their decisions are based on their "gut" – their instincts are good and they have a life-long track record of success based upon their reliance on intuition. They do not shrink from the tough calls; it is during times of high stress or instability and uncertainty that the wisdom and courage of directing leaders becomes most evident. These leaders are sensitive to the values and beliefs that drive their worldview and shudder at the notion of compromising their core values.

Like everyone, directing leaders have weaknesses. Among those are their disinterest in the minutiae of the process. They exhibit little patience for discussions about details and are not likely to labor over plans that address every possible contingency – although they often insist that those details be thought through and strategically addressed. When a directing leader is not accompanied by a more detail-oriented colleague, chaos results. Often you will find that directing leaders are great with large groups of people, but not especially warm with individuals. They also tend to be restless, have short attention spans, favor action over reflection, and may ignore financial limitations and realities. Their interest is in making good things happen – now – and they show little appetite for debating the ins and outs of the route that will get them where they need to go.

2. The STRATEGIC Leader

Newt Gingrich and Al Gore are typical strategic leaders. Generally speaking, these are individuals who are content to remain in the background, evaluating the options that lie before the organization, eventually developing detailed plans of action that address the key needs and opportunities. Strategic leaders are more comfortable at creating practical means of converting vision into action, than they are at pumping up the people with the big picture.

Strategic leaders are analysts of reality: they observe people and situations and collect empirical information, then run it through their mental grid to arrive at conclusions about the real conditions and opportunities of the world. They remain sufficiently detached to arrive at objective conclusions. Many strategic leaders view emotions and sensitivity as detrimental to the cause. Their allegiance is to truth and efficiency in making the vision reality.

Strategic leaders tend to be very thorough in their investigations and do not hesitate to ask the hard questions. They don't mind creating controversy because their primary quest is to understand reality so that they can develop a workable plan. Once they have amassed the facts and carefully analyzed them, strategic leaders are prone to developing creative, albeit sometimes complex, solutions.

These individuals are more loyal to the vision than they are to people. They also take great pride in being well-versed in their area of focus. It is rare to find a strategic leader who is at a loss to explain something; however, if they do not know the answer, such a deficiency fuels their zest for further discovery. Strategic leaders almost always over-prepare for meetings. Should you ask them a question, you are likely to get more detail than you care to hear – unless, of course, you, too, are a strategic leader.

Strategic leaders are typically seen as useful but they are generally not the most popular leaders. Because they focus on facts, figures, plans and possibilities, they are sometimes portrayed as being insensitive or unemotional, perhaps even robotic. The truth is that they do have feelings and they do care for people, but they know that they cannot trust feelings to arrive at useful conclusions. They are usually happier working with ideas than with people.

A common complaint about strategic leaders is that they take so long to arrive at decisions. This is frequently because they hate to make a decision without have complete information on which to base their judgment. These are people who believe they can eliminate all risks in decision-making if they can just analyze enough data. Unfortunately, nobody ever gets that much data. This tendency also points to a leaning toward perfectionism that sometimes undermines the efforts of the strategic leader.

3. The TEAM-BUILDING Leader

Directing leaders love the energy involved in chasing the dream. Strategic leaders love the intellectual challenge of understanding and planning. Team-building leaders love people. Their primary strength is their ability to interact with a wide variety of people and leave everyone feeling as if he/she has been heard, understood and loved. Team-building leaders are the best at mobilizing people around the vision through relational context.

These leaders love to organize people around a common cause. They work their relational network to bring together individuals who will share passion for the outcomes and who are likely to enjoy working together. In the process of building these new coalitions, they leave everyone feeling good about themselves, their team and the potential they have to produce something significant. The team-building leader is the life of the party – or, in the case of ministry activity, the popular, trusted friend of all whose charisma and personality encourage those in the trenches to give it their best shot.

Team-building leaders love people and hate paperwork. The stories are legion of such leaders who have made a shambles of well-constructed ministry strategies by simply ignoring anything that was put on paper – such as action plans, operational budgets, or ministry assignments and agendas. In fact, team-building leaders have a tendency to waffle on details, too. You will also find that their strength – relationships – is also their weakness because they often get burned by investing too much trust and confidence in people who do not (or, sometimes, cannot) pull through as promised.

4. The OPERATIONAL Leader

These individuals provide a degree of stability, predictability and consistency to the activity of the ministry. They focus upon the operations of the ministry – but they do so as leaders, not as managers. That's a major distinction. Managers lean toward maintaining and improving what exists; leaders emphasize creating new opportunities and solutions that result in breakthroughs. Operational leaders, then, conceive and introduce new routines designed to facilitate the accomplishment of the vision.

Operational leaders may be low-key and virtually invisible, but their contribution is indispensable. They devise systems that make things run smoothly. And, in the wake of the chaos and roadblocks generated by the other three types of leaders, a structural architect is needed to enable ministry to flow efficiently. The operational leader may also serve as the hub through which all activity is coordinated, to ensure that there are no loose ends, communication foibles or cost-overruns. In fact, these leaders provide the kind of attention to practical details that is rarely found in the activity of other types of leaders. It is the operational leader who often bears the bad financial news – but is rarely responsible for the difficulties that produced such difficulties.

By working on operational details every day, the operational leader sometimes loses sight of the fact that he/she is to be a leader not a manager. That role confusion can cause the leader to behave

85

more like a manager and lose sight of the vision in favor of simply running a well-oiled machine – regardless of where it is headed. That confusion can obviously hurt the ministry since it is the operational leader whose attention to detail often provides the financial, administrative or systemic correctives that facilitate ministry impact. Operational leaders, by nature, dislike conflict and will sometimes give in too easily in situations where a tough stand might result in an emotional battle. Other times, the manager in these people emerges such that they make choices that produce short-term results at the long-term expense of the ministry.

Four Distinct Types

Can you understand how teaming each of these four types of leaders together would give rise to a dynamic, multi-faceted hub of authority? And can you understand why few people possess more than one of these aptitudes?

And let's not lose sight of the other possibility that often arises in churches: teaming leaders who have the same aptitudes, rather than complementary aptitudes. Why would we do that? Because we're human; being with people who are just like us often feels comfortable and appropriate, but invariably leads to distress and disaster. Working intimately with people who possess divergent skills and views may produce better results, but it also makes us feel uncomfortable in the process of producing those outcomes. There is almost always a degree of productive tension among effective leadership teams because they are composed of people who approach the same problem differently. That creative tension is simply one of the positive building blocks that propels a well-matched team forward; remove the tension and you eliminate one of the strengths of the team.

Given the description of the leader-types provided above, think about the dynamics of having four directing leaders trying to work together on the same team. They all love the pressure of making tough calls, the public eye as they communicate the vision and direction, and the challenge of solving a vexing challenge. But get them together and take cover, because heated words and heavy objects will start flying when it comes time to make decisions or gain the attention of the public they serve!

What about bringing together four strategic leaders? Although they are less high-profile than the directing leaders, the strategic leaders also make for a toxic mix when combined. You can expect great documentation, insightful analysis and terrific planning, but don't hold your breath waiting for the congregation to willingly follow this group. Also realize that the plans might be sharp and well-communicated, but they are not likely to be embraced because the people don't trust this quartet. They are not likely to exhibit the people skills required to build a strong coalition around their clever plans.

If it's people skills you want, then why not enlist the services of a quartet of team-building leaders? Get four of these leaders together and they will provide you with a world-class love fest. Congregants will look forward to the fun-filled, high-connection gatherings they pull off. You might see some resources produced – telephone directories, new Rolodex cards, a calendar of future events – but don't count on much progress toward the vision.

Blending a handful of operational leaders would result in a tidy, efficient meeting, with a carefully designed process – but without the heart or inspiration needed to stimulate followers to jump into the fray. People would know what they are expected to do, they would understand the details involved in carrying out their job, there would be ample assessment and progress reports, but after a while congregants would lose sight of the big picture and simply feel like they are part of a well-oiled machine that is in maintenance mode.

So the conclusion to draw is that merely piecing together a group of warm bodies who are capable of working together – even if they agree on specific outcomes – is not likely to produce optimal results. Teams work best when they are comprised of individuals whose personal abilities and gifts contribute value while their personal deficiencies are compensated for via the abilities and efforts of other team members.

Teams Can Be Fragile

We have to be realistic about this, of course. While the teaming of these four types may produce incredible results, it also facilitates dynamic tension and occasional conflict. That tension will never disappear, since each leader-type has a unique perspective on leadership and the vision, and brings divergent skills, thinking styles and contextual perspectives to the table. If that tension can be properly managed, it is one of the sparks that keeps the team growing, innovating and charging forward. That tension creates a positive energy if it can be appropriately harnessed.

Consider one other critical insight: if the team is lacking one or more of these leader-types, the team will be missing a necessary component in its efforts to facilitate transformation. No one of these leaders is more important than any other – although we typically praise the directing leader and take the others for granted – but no one of those leaders will be successful without the partnership of the other types. As you reflect on the implications of this, keep in mind that this division of skills, focus and energy explains why so many solo leaders feel overwhelmed, burned out and incapable of leading effectively.

The key to effective team leadership, then, is having multiple leaders with *complementary* aptitudes working together, regardless of the size of the church or the nature of the ministry they are leading. Leadership teams that have these four types working cooperatively are needed to lead not just the entire church, but departments and programs within the ministry too – and that means identifying a wealth of leaders to integrate into the leadership process.[1]

Team Skills

If you have ever tried working in a team environment, then you know that it is more complex than simply throwing four gifted leaders with complementary talents together and expecting them to create synergistic results. Just as a family produces group dynamics that must be understood and strategically managed, so must a leadership team be comprised of individuals who are willing to work hard at making the team a healthy unit.

In practice, one of the most important attributes of an effective team leader is the commitment to serving not only the church, but the other leader as well. This invariably requires a willingness to sacrifice personal rewards and resources for the good of the team and the accomplishment of its goals. An individual who approaches the team as a platform for personal accomplishment is not likely to add value to the ministry. An individual who views the team as a means of maximizing his/her personal contribution will undoubtedly prove to be an asset – as long as that view is not based on using the team as a stepping stone to personal notoriety.

Teams also need partners who respect and believe in each other. Without a firm conviction that the leadership partners can be trusted to make good decisions, to protect each others' best interests and to remain focused on the vision rather than personal glory, the team will go nowhere, regardless of how gifted and experienced each of the members may be. Leaders take risks; it is difficult to pursue risks if you do not trust the motives or abilities of others to make appropriate choices or to provide support. If a deep level of trust does not exist, team members are not likely to rely upon each others' judgment or capabilities when key moments arise.

Each team member must be committed to increasing his/her expertise within the domain that they represent in the team mix. This means a commitment to constant learning through whatever means will raise their capacity level: reading, classes, being mentored, case studies, etc. If one member slacks off, the entire team suffers as a result. An obligation of leadership is to take your responsibility seriously; an obligation of being in a team is to support your colleagues by pulling your weight. Personal growth in leadership thus becomes a lifelong challenge.

Teams that acknowledge their special significance to the ministry they serve and appreciate their shared history last longer and produce better results than those that lack a sense of their uniqueness and inimitable experience. That realization should cause the team to feel an uncommon bond.

Not Everyone Is A Leader

For the sake of clarity, let me point out that most people will not participate in ministry leadership. This is because most people are not leaders. Our research suggests that more than four out of every five believers is primarily a follower. Naturally, everyone provides leadership at some times in his/her life, but by inclination and gifting most people are followers who need to be led and who will contribute to the cause of Christ by using the other gifts and skills they possess. People who are leaders are neither better nor worse than followers; all of us have a significant role to play in the unfolding of the kingdom, no matter what that role may be. As Paul wrote:

Just as each of us has one body with many members, and these members do not all have the same function, so in Christ do we who are many form one body, and each member belongs to all the others. We have different gifts, according to the grace given us. (Romans 12:4-6)

Be careful that you do not assume that everyone who says he/ she is a leader is telling the truth. Our surveys find that most people – roughly three out of five adults, and an even greater proportion of teenagers – claim that they are leaders. That, of course, is a gross overestimation. We learned that people like the image of being a leader, but not the responsibilities, the constant criticism, and the hard work that is involved in leading. Most people do not have the wisdom and discernment, nor the courage, to consistently make wise, strategic, tough choices, and to stand by those choices.

In the end, an effective leadership team is comprised of people who sacrifice their own notoriety and power because they believe they have been called to serve as a leader, because they are demonstrating godly character, and because they want to blend their skills and abilities with those who can add value to the mix. In great teams each partner makes a significant and necessary contribution to the end result. Because each person pulls his/her own weight in the relationship, there is a sense of interdependence, equality and mutual respect that fortifies the determination of the group to overcome the odds and make the vision real.

FOOTNOTES

[1] Perhaps you are wondering how to easily determine a person's leadership aptitude without having to rely upon trail and error. In 2001, upon the completion of the beta testing phase, Barna Research will be releasing the Ministry Leader Profile, a self-administered diagnostic tool that will enable individuals to evaluate their leadership potential. The tool will explore a person's calling, character, competencies and leadership aptitude. For information about the availability of this resource, check the Barna Research Group website, at www.barna.org.

CHAPTER SIX

THE PROCESS
BEHIND SUCCESSFUL
TEAM LEADERSHIP

When you watch a great organization at work, everything looks easy. The mission and vision of the organization are clear and attractive, the people seem to gladly and effortlessly fulfill their responsibilities, and impressive results appear to emerge on cue. Having worked with Fortune 500 companies, government agencies, political campaigns and non-profit organizations, as well as churches and parachurch ministries, I have been privileged to get a glimpse behind the curtain at what it really takes for such results to occur. As you might imagine, great outcomes do not happen by chance: there is inevitably a sophisticated, intentional and strategic process that propels the organization forward.

To conduct research for this book we dug beneath the surface of several dozen churches across the country where effective lay leadership teams are in place. Unfortunately, there was no standard formula and no magic process that was employed across-the-board. In fact, no two churches had identical processes for developing their team system. Even their underlying philosophies of leadership and lay participation in ministry showed noteworthy variances. But we were able to identify a substantial and significant group of common practices – "best practices," if you will – that enabled these churches to emerge from the pack.

It is worth noting that our research even uncovered a trio of expected, but important observations about the team leadership process in these ministries. First, leaders serving in these churches get great pleasure and satisfaction from leading within a team context. Second, the churches have a measurably broader ministry impact than do churches that do not rely upon lay leadership teams. Third, the potential for continued numerical growth is virtually unlimited – and the churches we studied are, in fact, exploding with numerical growth.

Churches that emphasize lay leadership teams share a variety of characteristics (i.e., the best practices) that fall into four general categories. First, there are specific ways in which they create a viable leadership partnership. Second, they develop an environment designed to facilitate effective team leadership. Third, the ways in which the leaders perform their duties reflect some similarities. Fourth, lay leaders are intentionally set-up to succeed in their roles. Each of these elements bears further exposition.

Leadership Partnerships

Leadership is about people serving people, so we ought to begin a discussion of the process by understanding how the people component operates in these churches. Without appropriate software (i.e,, people), it doesn't matter how sophisticated your hardware (i.e., systems and resources) might be: nothing will be produced.

It all starts with an appropriate team design, i.e., knowing what type of people are desirable, and how to incorporate those people into a true partnership. This is the philosophical end of the process: determining the proper number of people to invite into leadership teams (usually no more than six), specifying the criteria by which individuals are invited to become team members, defining the roles of each participant, describing the relationship between lay leaders and pastoral staff, fixing the term of service for team members, conceptualizing the training regimen for leaders, and so forth. These might seem like irrelevant details, but addressing these issues early in the process allows the church and its leaders to focus on the important issues once the system is triggered.

Great teams are the result of intelligent recruiting. Just as a basketball team becomes successful because its scouts and executives have done their homework and carefully planned their draft choices and trades to accumulate a roster of talented players who possess complementary skills, so do churches recruit high-potential lay leaders with the intent of developing their talent and matching them with complementary leaders. They look for a range of attributes that suggest the likelihood of leadership impact: a definable leadership aptitude, a teachable spirit, mature faith, passion for the vision, a servant's heart, and basic competencies.

Once these individuals have been identified and recruited, they must be strategically blended into a team in which their contribution will multiply the team's impact. Herein emerged one of the more interesting distinctions between churches that effectively match lay leaders and those that do not. The churches that create ineffective teams tend to match people on the basis of personality, assuming that personality conflicts represent doom for a team. The churches that succeed with lay teams, though, considered personality to be of minimal importance. The criteria on which they matched lay leaders was passion for the same vision, followed by complementary leadership aptitudes, then levels of experience in leadership, and only then did personality come under consideration.

It was rare to find that these churches rejected an otherwise viable match solely on the basis of personality. Why? "We're dealing with spiritually mature people here," explained the senior pastor of a church that has dozens of thriving lay leadership teams – none of which were developed around personality traits and styles. "The key to success is that they are sold out to the vision and that they have skills that fit together well. Sure, we have some dicey moments when some of these high performance, on-edge personalities first get together, but we have never yet had a serious battle. The common ground is the vision and the desire to serve. If we can help our leaders to focus on those things, they get over the personality stuff."

Once the individuals have been joined into a team, churches encourage them to spend time gelling as a close-knit, single-minded service unit. This means figuring out how to collaborate. My observation of the process indicates that there are several common themes that churches employ to facilitate collaboration. One thread is that of creating biblical community within the team. The team is positioned to provide personal identity; a sense of belonging to something meaningful; status or prestige; and relational intimacy with peers. Another thread is that of developing unity: no matter how heated the internal disagreements may get, or how diverse the members' points of view might be, once the team emerges from behind closed doors they embrace one unified view. A related theme is that the team must arrive at a means of making cooperative decisions based on the diversity of talents, experiences and gifts resident within the group. Yet another outcome to be achieved is that the team members find the delicate balance between maintaining their personal independence while developing a satisfying dependence upon each other. All of these developments won't accomplish much unless there is genuine mutual respect among members.

Identifying those hallowed outcomes is a first step toward seeing them become a reality. The process of facilitating those outcomes varied considerably, but typically involved mentoring and oversight from a pastor during the initial stage of the group's life, with that responsibility for shepherding the process being transferred to the team captain within a short period. In fact, one of the factors often used in selecting a team captain was their ability to help the team become a truly collaborative unit.

A key to the process was for the team to draw up a written covenant. The scope of these agreements ranged from a simple, one-page commitment to serve God, team members, and the church in accordance with specified biblical principles and a standard of personal excellence, to multi-page, detailed documents that covered a broad array of practices and perspectives. Among the items that team covenants encompassed were the vision; plans; goals; strategies; standards of behavior; methods of accountability; penalties for failure to live up to the agreement; member tenure; and specific personal spiritual growth needs and commitments.

At first it seemed to me that such documents took the whole arrangement too far. But after studying the effect of these covenants, their value became clear. "When I signed that covenant," recalled one lay leader at a large Methodist church, "I really had to stop and think about what I was agreeing to do. There's something about putting your name on the dotted line that gives the agreement a real seriousness that seems more real than simply talking through some points of agreement and giving verbal assent." Many lay leaders admitted that they occasionally return to the covenant to study it, hoping that they have not failed to keep up their responsibilities.

A final aspect of the people element is choosing a captain for the team. Once again, this may seem like a minor detail that is hardly worth mentioning, but it turns out to be a highly significant task that can make or break the health and impact of the team. This element is so important that I will devote the entire next chapter to the process of selecting the captain.

An Environment for Team Leadership

Team success is somewhat dependent on the environment they are provided for leadership. While we witnessed some cases in which the environment was hostile to teams and yet they succeeded in spite of that obstacle, the more common observation was that churches that dared teams to overcome the environment rarely had healthy and effective teams in place. The wisest strategy is for a church to intentionally clear the path for teams so that they have the greatest opportunity possible to experience success.

Setting teams up for victory means that there must be a culture that supports lay leadership teams. There are numerous examples of cultural conditioning for team impact. Customs such as expecting all leadership to be conducted by teams, encouraging laity to assume key leadership posts, and deferring decisions until the appropriate team has made a choice are examples of cultural posturing for team success. Symbols of the importance of teams include the titles given to team-based leaders ("lay minister," "ministry director," and "lay pastor" are examples), requiring leadership teams to develop the church budget (rather than having pastoral staff make those determinations), and taking time in corporate events, such as worship services and congregational meetings, to introduce the congregation to each team and its members.

Many churches revised their values statements to reflect the significance of the team approach. For instance, some of the values specified included the notions that key ministry decisions are to be made by lay leadership teams, that team leadership is esteemed more highly than solo leadership, and that the church is responsible for preparing team leaders for positive experiences. Churches rewrote their constitutions to describe their decision-making process as being team-based; others introduced program development and accountability systems that were based on teams conceiving, implementing and evaluating such ministry efforts. All of these instances were designed to communicate an inescapable truth: the church lives and dies by its lay leadership teams.

Preparing the internal context (i.e., the church culture) represents only one side of the coin. The other side relates to the external context – the world culture and its impact on the church's ministry. For the leadership teams to reach their potential, they must understand the challenges and opportunities in the world we have been called to inhabit and influence. Facilitating such analysis and interpretation, in relation to the church's vision and strategic thrust, will not only shape the choices of the ministry but also determine whether or not the teams will optimize their influence both inside and outside of the church.

A team that thrives must coalesce around a significant challenge. Leaders tend to be busy, intelligent, skilled, active people. Unless they have a serious challenge before them – and, in the case of team-based leadership, ones that clearly transcend the ability of each individual member, working alone, to meet those challenges – then the team will never rise to its loftiest potential. Leaders' adrenaline pumps when it seems that the challenge is implausible to master. The team truly revs up to full gear when there is a sense of urgency added to the magnitude of the challenge.

Every great team holds itself accountable to standards of behavior, as well as performance goals. The evaluation process is handled as objectively as possible, often involving the help of an outsider (e.g., a staff member familiar with the work of the group) and designed to reflect the highest levels of integrity. Great teams know that you only improve what you measure; and that you should only bother to measure that which is meaningful in light of your vision.

It was interesting to realize that teams do not carry out such accountability once a year, as if they were reviewing the job performance of an employee who was due for a raise or promotion. The teams we watched were consistently asking themselves tough questions about all levels of team activity; questions related to quality, strategy, community, pace, passion, image, productivity, stewardship, and so forth. How pleasing it was to recognize that the self-accountability process became second nature to these teams in short order. And the accountability process cut two ways: first, they evaluate the team itself, and second, they regularly evaluated each other, as contributors to the team effort. This determination to do the right things and to do them right was refreshing and challenging.

High-Level Performance

For great leadership to transpire, the team must engage in specific activities. Besides providing leadership – the motivating, mobilizing, directing and resourcing of people so that their shared vision can be accomplished – the team must behave in certain ways to generate such outcomes.

For instance, we found that highly effective teams worked on facilitating outstanding communication. Sometimes the relationships and information flow occur naturally, but often the team must focus on intentionally enabling good communication to happen. One aspect of this art was to ensure that the team has frequent times for interaction, whether that be via scheduled meetings or telephone appointments, or through the use of tools such as e-mail. Encouraging team members to listen carefully to what each other has to say is another tactic that we saw enforced. An outcome of the team's emphasis upon community and collaboration was the development of an environment in which everyone was expected to contribute useful insights. Openness to everyone's input is critical to fostering understanding and excellence, as well as the sense that each person adds value to the team. As will be discussed in the next chapter, the captain was frequently the individual who made sure that the communication process was healthy within the team.

A team that is afraid to take risks is a team that will not serve its constituency well. Leadership is about making choices; always taking the safest route will limit the potential of the ministry. Naturally, a team should not be reckless in its decision-making, but neither should it limit the ministry because it is scared to try something and fail. The best teams are those that take measured risks and, if the risk does not pay-off, learn from those failures so that future decisions are better and more productive. When a team lacks reasonable caution or consistently makes inadvisable choices, then it may be time for the groups' overseer (often the pastor or a staff person) to provide tighter guidance on its operations. The overseer may need to portray the recent decisions as failures, clearly define the objectives and standards by which the team should operate or change either the captain or the individuals on the team in order to raise the performance level of the group.

Successful teams are disciplined. That means they have a narrow focus. In many churches where teams exist but are ineffective, a major reason is that they are expected to lead in areas that extend well beyond the boundaries of their charter or expertise. Great teams are not the savior of the church; they have a narrow, well-defined focus and stick to their niche. One of the captain's greatest contributions to the team is to help it say "no" to great opportunities, simply because those opportunities will divert the team's attention and resources from the very outcomes that it exists to produce.

For example, a team that exists to lead the worship function within a church would be ill-advised to also step in to a troubled Christian education program and try to solve its problems. Some observers will argue that this is foolish: a strong team should serve wherever its services are needed, and people can handle more than one task at a time. Logical as that may sound, the track record of teams shows that they are effective when they zero in on one major challenge at a time, one in which they share a common vision and passion.

These are not teams built on a business model that implores the team to take whatever work it can get to generate revenue; they are based on a passion model that expects team members to exploit their gifts, abilities and experiences to empower the church within a dimension of ministry about which the team members are passionate. Focusing on multiple areas of ministry will likely dissipate their time, resources, and skills, causing them to produce less effective outcomes in their primary area of concentration. Consequently, the entire church will be worse off for their involvement in the additional area since now their primary area of service will suffer from neglect and their mastery of the new dimension will also be limited by their passion, vision and capacity.

One interesting observation was that some team-driven churches have tried to bridge the gap between narrow focus and broad needs by creating one or a handful of "consultant" teams whose primary function is to step in to help fix daunting problems or to address unusual challenges in a range of ministry areas within the church. The passion of the leaders in those teams is to provide help where help is needed to raise the ministry to its highest level. When a church has leaders who are willing to lead in this type of as-needed role, and to devote themselves to learning whatever is needed to provide excellence within a variety of functions, this tactic can work well.

No matter what the focus of a team is, though, success requires flexibility in the team's efforts. Because effective teams monitor their progress as they serve, there are constant mid-course adjustments being made. Rigidity undermines leadership. Because we lead people in dynamic environments, continual learning and recalibration are crucial to getting the job done with efficiency, impact and excellence.

High performance happens within the team when everyone shares the responsibility and makes significant contributions. You can tell if a team shares responsibility by their approach to problem solving. If the conversations regarding solutions become one-person dialogues regarding appropriate action to take, chances are good that the coalition is a work group rather than a team – that is, a collection of subordinates who dutifully and mindlessly take their orders from a chief. Great teams rely upon each person to lend his/ her experience and expertise to developing creative and viable solutions to each challenge they face. If even one of the team members is frozen out of that chain of interaction, the entire team is crippled.

Measurable goals are one of the most important components existent in the team's operations. Goals focus the team on what is important while also giving the group a benchmark against which to compare its productivity and impact. Teams that meet their goals have reason to celebrate and set their sights higher. Teams that fail to reach their goals automatically receive a sense of their weaknesses and may then apply their problem-solving skills to their internal operations. We did note that teams lacking goals also lack the same level of energy and focus that is evident within goal-driven teams.

A final factor that is critical to the health and impact of leadership teams is being spiritual centered. Every great team we studied prays together regularly, and the members pray daily about the team's responsibilities and performance. This emphasis on prayer was one of the indications of how seriously team members take their involvement in ministry leadership and their esteem of the team approach. Beyond prayer, we also found that the leadership action and problem-solving approach of effective teams leans heavily on the Bible for guidance, in terms of the principles considered as solutions and the behavioral parameters of the team.

The emphasis on spirituality is critical since leaders serve as role models for people, whether they want to or not. Within the church, the ways in which ministry is done may have as big an impact on congregants' lives as the strategies and tactics employed by leaders may have on the life of the church. Teams should take their cues from Jesus and the disciples, or from Paul and his disciples: prayer and reference to biblical principles were integrated into the decision-making process. That approach clearly influenced the early church, as described in Acts.

Equipped for Impact

No matter how skilled and experienced your leaders are, they need some forms of assistance to maximize their leadership potential. Effective leaders and leadership teams are always learning and growing. We discovered that team-led churches strive to push their teams to their developmental limit.

Every one of the churches we examined that uses teams to great effect provides leadership training on a regular basis. In some cases this constitutes a weekly, one-hour meeting in which there is time for teaching, dialogue, reporting and relationships. In other churches, the process takes place monthly or quarterly. (The most common strategy was to have a monthly leadership development event, scheduled for the same duration at the same time each month – e.g., from 9 a.m. to noon on the third Saturday of every month.)

Because these churches recognize that leaders learn from many experiences and in a variety of ways, developmental efforts are broad-based. Each church creates its own unique means of helping leaders grow, but there were two principles that described each of these churches.

First, they do not limit their training to lectures in a classroom. In most of these churches, the expert divulging useful information to leaders was heavily front-loaded and then used sparingly once the leader was in full gear. In other words, when an individual initially joins the leadership family at the church, there is often an intensive introductory training regimen that utilizes the lecture approach, but once that orientation process is completed, the training process is more interactive and individualized. Churches contextualize the training to account for the unique conditions and opportunities that define the church's ministry.

Second, these churches strive to elevate the performance of their leaders through a wide variety of training approaches. Even though many people have had extensive leadership training in the secular world, leading a business and leading a church are not the same. The same skills might be used, but it is imperative to differentiate some of the nuances, such as the difference between bottom-line thinking and having a servant mindset. A typical team-driven church offers leaders at least a half dozen ways of learning during the course of the year. Among those approaches are the following options:

1. Regular self-assessment, leading to a personal growth plan. Because effectiveness demands a sense of quality, these churches expect leaders to measure themselves in key areas – character in particular, but competencies and outcomes, too – and to pinpoint areas of strength and weakness. Great leaders maximize their strengths but recognize and attack their weaknesses to expand their capacity. Standardized tools may be used in this process, such as spiritual gifts tests, leadership inventories or church evaluation profiles, with special attention devoted to the areas in which the individual is providing focused leadership.

2. Many churches provide a mentoring or coaching program for all of their leaders. In many churches the pastor and other staff members serve as "master mentors," with some of the mature lay leaders coaching less experienced lay leaders. This apprenticeship model is one of the most effective methods of expanding the numbers of leaders available to the church, while also fortifying the ability to pass on the ministry's culture and strategies with a minimum of effort.

3. Formal, classroom style instruction about leadership is almost universal – although most churches strive to make their classroom experiences times of facilitated discussion rather than note-taking lectures. These meetings are used to regularly bring leaders back to the basics – e.g., the church's mission, vision and values – as well as to provide information on methods and perspective.

4. Agenda-less events – described by one leader as "purposeful social events" – are designed to facilitate dialogue among leaders. While clergy are typically overworked, lay leaders are also busy people, generally juggling their occupation, their family and their church responsibilities. There may be few, non-accidental opportunities for lay leaders to interact with all of the other leaders in the church without an oppressive agenda lurking in the shadows. Providing team members the chance to find out what other teams are doing, what they're experiencing and learning, and to maintain personal connections often produce unpredictable but invaluable results for the ministry. Since leaders are problem solvers, these occasional connections with other leaders stimulate creative thinking and cross-team solutions that otherwise might not have occurred.

5. Many churches try to keep their leaders up to date on the latest and most helpful leadership resources. Some churches accomplish this by identifying useful resources for leaders and leaving it up to the individual to pursue the

resource if and when their time and interest allows that pursuit. In other cases the church carves time out of the regularly scheduled leadership meetings to call attention to key resources and to describe one or more valuable lessons that can be drawn from the resource. Some churches go so far as to acquire and distribute the book, tape or article in question to each leader, and instruct them to digest the information and share their thoughts about it at an upcoming leaders meeting. The underlying desire, regardless of the approach, is to motivate church leaders to stay fresh and current in their thinking about leadership.

6. Experience-based learning has proven to have impressive influence in people's lives. Whether it be a "ropes course," some other type of adventure-based, team-building experience, or any other real-world experience that conveys leadership lessons through hands-on participation, the more progressive (and larger) churches have recently begun focusing more attention on this means of development.

7. "Road trips rule!" Such was the exuberant exclamation of one young leader who noted that he learns more from attending seminars and conferences in the company of fellow leaders, and having time to discuss the insights delivered in those events with his peers than from any other developmental process in which he engages. He is not alone in that sentiment. Getting perspective from high-caliber, external experts can be a challenging and invigorating experience. The landscape is filled with ministry-oriented training events these days. Team-based churches often have a budget for taking a number of leaders to such events. One of the newest twists on this approach is the use of satellite-delivered training through which respected leaders broadcast their insights to a large number of churches (i.e., downlink sites) at which as many leaders as want to participate can to experience the teaching.[1]

One important view held by team-led churches – and verified by team members themselves – is that it is crucial to provide continual training and experiences for leaders to stay challenged, growing and sharp. In spite of their busy lives, a majority of lay leaders we interviewed across the country said they want more training in leadership competencies and that they want that training to come from their church. This underscores the concept of the senior pastor being a leader of leaders, rather than striving to be the dominant spiritual leader in the life of every congregant.

One of the ancillary benefits of providing regular training for lay leaders is that it reinforces people's commitment to serving the church through leadership. Always keep in mind that as satisfying as leadership may be to those who practice this art within the church, lay leaders are under enormous pressure at work, at home, and in their personal relationships. Leadership, by its very nature, is difficult; a church cannot afford to take these people for granted. Like any human being trying to make his/her life count, leaders can get discouraged and therefore need to be loved and appreciated. Such recognition of their contribution, and celebration of the victories they achieve along the way, does much to reinforce their participation as a leader.

The Marks of Success

Perhaps this goes without saying, but success in leadership must be acknowledged and reinforced. What happens when a church has effective teams leading the way? People's lives are changed: increasing numbers of individuals become more Christ-like in various ways. This is the primary function of leaders – to see people's lives transformed in conjunction with the vision for change that the Lord has conveyed to the church. It is only natural that the primary point of assessment would relate to life change.

Great teamwork also produces a church that enjoys rich community. Ministry is about people and their relationships with

God and with each other. Effective leadership enables people to enjoy deeper and more enriching interaction. Naturally, another outcome is that the specific goals set by the team are accomplished – some of which will relate specifically to transformation and relationships, but others of which may be more narrowly focused. Another result to look for is evidence of self-evaluation occurring – at the individual, team and congregational levels. The church that does not constantly assess how it is doing is a church that will seduce itself into believing that affirmative anecdotes and self-generated praise represent reality. Effective teams know better than to fall into that trap.

Earlier I promised to look more carefully at another key role in this process: the function of the captain. Let's now turn our attention to that role.

FOOTNOTES

[1] There are two ways in which satellite-based training is available these days. One option is to experience the singular, topical events broadcast by ministries such as Willow Creek Community Church, Saddleback Community Church, and Injoy. An alternative that delivers valuable continuity and breadth is provided by organizations like the Church Communications Network, which offer a series of monthly or bi-monthly broadcasts on topics of interest to church leaders, as well as special pay-per-view types of training events. More information on CCN's programming can be obtained from their website (www.ccnonline.net) or by calling them at 1-800-321-6781.

CHAPTER SEVEN

THE **CAPTAIN**:
THE TEAM'S POINT PERSON

On sports teams, the position of captain is often ceremonial, a post awarded to the team's star performer or to someone who has served the team well for many years. Often, that role comes with limited responsibility: leading the team out of the locker room, representing the team during the pre-game coin toss to see who gets first possession of the ball, conveying referees' decisions to the rest of the team, and so forth.

In business and ministry, however, where the fate of the organization is dependent upon the quality of the leadership provided, the role of the team captain is far from being an empty commendation. Although the captain is one of several leaders on the team, the selection of the captain often makes or breaks a team. While a top-flight captain does not make the entire team great, a mediocre captain can hinder the performance of an otherwise effective team.

One of the more surprising outcomes from my research on effective leadership teams in churches was that every successful team we observed had a captain in place. The job was not merely ceremonial, either; the captain proved to be the pivot on which the team revolved. That person was more than just a warm and willing body who called team meetings and arrived early to make sure the coffee was warm by the starting time. Captains add value to the team, even though they are just one partner in the leadership collective.

Why Teams Need A Captain

Perhaps it seems that having a captain on a team of leaders is unnecessarily inviting dissension – that is, the selection of one person to oversee or direct the energies of the team might be unhappily interpreted by the other leaders as singling out the captain as "the best leader" or the most important person in the group.

To the contrary, my exploration of leadership teams showed that the role of the captain was accepted as necessary by team members – if the role was properly described and positioned. In essence, the captain is the facilitator of the team's process. Teams become busy doing their work, and someone must serve as the traffic cop to ensure that necessary efforts are neither overlooked nor hindered by unproductive or inappropriate group dynamics.

How does a captain capably perform this duty of keeping the team focused, productive and mutually supportive – without derailing his/her own unique leadership contribution to the common cause they have agreed to pursue? This individual must have the ability to balance two unique roles – the specialization that he/she provides in the leadership mix (e.g., representing one of the four leadership aptitudes) as well as the function of a process facilitator. To faithfully carry out this role, the captain juggles leadership within the ministry focus and ministry to his/her fellow leaders.

Primary Ways
the Captain Leads the Team

1. MAINTAINS THE TEAM'S FOCUS ON THE VISION.
Someone must attach the blinders to the vision of the team. The chances are good that there will be numerous opportunities for the team to accomplish positive tangible outcomes along the way that have nothing to do with the vision around which the team was brought together. The captain is responsible for aligning the team with its vision day after day, identifying alluring alternatives

as mere distractions from the true goal of the team. The captain may not be the main vision-caster of the group, but he/she ought to be the primary champion of the vision within the group. If a team loses sight of its reason for existence, the captain has failed the team, and the team will fail the church.

2. FACILITATES POSITIVE AND PRODUCTIVE RELATION-SHIPS AMONG TEAM MEMBERS. A team must move together in unison if it is to reach its goals. Such progress demands good relationships among the members. However, the aggressive, strong-willed, independent nature of most leaders results in tenuous interaction unless someone assumes the role of "negotiator" among the members. This means that a great captain is one who maintains a good working relationship with each member and is also capable of sensing impending relational danger and helping the team to avoid counterproductive engagement. Captains empower members to provide their views and add to the team mix without feeling that they are being overpowered by others.

3. IDENTIFIES OPPORTUNITIES FOR INDIVIDUAL GROWTH. Ideally, each team member is continually in the process of becoming a better leader and disciple. The captain powers that developmental emphasis by encouraging efforts to grow, by recognizing growth that is evident, by identifying specific aspects of a leader's character or competencies that require improvement, or by informing a leader of upcoming opportunities for useful training or education. This might entail alerting a team member to classes, noting new resources that are available and might be of value, or discussing personal leadership weaknesses that the individual may not be aware of and needs to address. The ultimate goal is for the captain to motivate each team member to consistently be striving to grow as a leader and as a follower of Christ.

4. PREPARES THE TEAM TO MOVE AHEAD BY ACQUIRING RESOURCES. A team without resources will not get too far.

The captain strives to pave the way toward progress by generating the resources necessary for sustained movement by the team. This might relate to human resources, financial resources, or other components needed to move the ministry closer to fulfilling the vision. To satisfy this endeavor, a captain must therefore stay well-informed of what each team member will be doing in relation to the team's ends and anticipate the resources that will be needed to produce the intended outcomes.

5. DEMONSTRATES PERSONAL LEADERSHIP PRODUCTIVITY. Assuming the position of captain does not exempt the individual from the need to carry his/her own weight within the team's activity. To maintain the respect of team members as well as the balance of skills and competencies within the group, the captain must continue to produce the outcomes that the team requires of him/her. Failure to keep up with his/her colleagues will undermine the captain's standing. In the eyes of team members, the captain is a team member first, a captain second. The most important outcome from the captain must be whatever specialized outcomes the team leans on the willingness to provide, regardless of being captain.

Can a team operate effectively without a captain? Yes, but not without someone filling that role. In some ministries an outside ministry professional – such as a pastor or staff member – serves as a surrogate captain. Usually, this approach keeps the team from operating at peak effectiveness, though, because the outsider has neither a complete understanding of the team's activity and temperament, nor the complete trust of the team members. While having an outsider serve as the captain is often better than not having any at all, the ideal is to have a team member pull double-duty – serving both as a fully productive group member as well as the team's captain. Further, I have seen that when a church uses a pastor or staff person in the captain's position, an underlying reason is often to preserve control over what the team is doing – and that can be more debilitating than operating without a captain.

Here's a word of warning, too. While Directing Leaders usually assume that they should be the team's leader, they often make terrible captains because of their lack of detail orientation and their insensitivity to the quirks of other members. Strategic Leaders are good with details, but generally lack the people skills to serve effectively in this role. Team-building Leaders provide the interpersonal encouragement that is often needed to complement the delivery of bad news, but those individuals often lack the focus on specifics and the commitment to plans that shape effective team development. In the end, you may discover the Operational Leader is your best bet as a captain, especially since they are typically process people and the captain's position is a process role.

The Making of a Great Captain

Leaders are born, but captains are appointed and refined. No matter how an individual assumes the captaincy, there are certain functions that make a person shine in this role.

A person is not likely to perform the job well unless he/she understands the captain's role. Simply put, that role is to be the chief servant of the team. In addition to facilitating outcomes and group health, the captain always has an eye on how to build up the team's members and the team itself. I noted that in many cases, the individual who serves as the coach or overseer of the team – usually a pastor or staff person – would invest additional time and energy mentoring the captain as to the nature of the captain's role. This investment is heaviest in the early life of the group and during the formative months of the person's tenure as captain.

Great captains never trumpet their position as captain. The captain simply accepts the added responsibilities as one way in which he/she can help to insure the success of the team as it pursues God's vision for them. A great captain is one who blends in with the rest of the members, always remembering that the team is the hero – not an individual in the group – and that the team retains control in each situation. Being effective in the role of captain demands a sensitive balance between providing guidance and control; the likely outcome of providing leadership to a team member, as captain, determines how far to go, how strong to be, or how much to back off.

To faithfully execute the role of captain, though, the individual must wholeheartedly believe in the people on the team and the vision that they are pursuing. Anything less than complete trust in and respect for the team members will result in favoritism and an innate unwillingness to provide total support to each member equally and unequivocally. Failure to own the vision will undermine the captain's commitment to the team members, team process and ministry outcomes. A captain who is not completely sold out to the vision and to the team will eventually harm the team – either intentionally or unintentionally.

In the process of helping the team reach its potential, the captain must demonstrate loving and respectful patience with members and with the team process. In some ways, this reflects invaluable modeling for internal team dynamics. By learning from and building upon the unique contributions of each team member, the captain silently teaches each one to appreciate both the value of teamwork and the worth of each team member as a person and leader.

Leadership teams are similar to a marriage in many respects, demanding time to foster a deep relationship among the partners, unity of perspective and the furtherance and protection of mutual best interests. Our research on divorce also emphasizes that poor communication is one of the major reasons why marriages falter. Captains maximize their leadership to the team by optimizing the communication process of the team. Effective captains listen carefully, constantly and completely – keeping the flow of communication consistent, hearing what is not being said as well as what is said, and clarifying the content of messages conveyed. While all leaders need to be good communicators to be effective, the tendency among leaders will be to tell others what to do or how to do it, without always listening to what others are saying – even partners in leadership.

Captains protect the team against this kind of one-sided communication that destroys relationships.

Captains also serve the team by encouraging the group to push until it reaches its highest level of performance and productivity. Without someone on the inside standing guard against slippage of standards, the chances are good that leaders will do whatever they need to do to get by and move on. Captains represent the line of defense against settling for whatever gets by. Great leadership redefines the boundaries of success and excellence. Great captains push their teams to live up to the highest performance standards they can possibly satisfy, without lowering the bar when things get tough.

Along the way, captains encourage their teams to take plausible risks. A team that does not risk will not lead people very far. The natural tendency of teams – especially those that are newly formed or are seeking to make their mark in ministry – is to follow the safe path and accept whatever progress can be achieved without risking failure. Great captains motivate the team to push themselves to the point of maximum output. Sometimes the results will catapult the ministry forward; other times, all-out effort brings forth failure. However, captains can help their team to use failure as a step to success, dissecting the undesirable results to learn insights that will serve the team as it takes new ground in future forays.

In the end, a valuable captain is like adding another member to the team without having to recruit, train and integrate another person to the dynamics. The captain accepts the role with humility, fulfills the role with energy and wisdom, and enhances the team through his/her servanthood. A great captain always remembers that the role is about the health of the team, not about the ascendancy of the captain to greater heights of glory and reputation. The captain succeeds only when the team succeeds; no matter how competent and superbly he/she serves the team as its captain, if the team fails, the captain also fails. Such an all-for-one-and-one-for-all philosophy prohibits the team from succumbing to blaming others for their shortcomings, offering excuses for their problems, or accomplishing results by lowering their standards.

Selecting the Captain

One of the most counter-intuitive lessons derived from my exploration of leadership teams was how churches usually select their team captains. It seemed reasonable to expect the team to assemble, assess themselves, and determine whom they would most like to follow as their captain.

To the contrary, I discovered that the process seems to work best when the captain is chosen for the team by an outside force – usually by the senior pastor or the staff person to whom the team will report. While this initially may seem like heavy-handed domination, this process does work well if the individual who selects the captain truly comprehends the significance and the role of the position.

Let's assume that the pastor determines the captain. This makes sense because the pastor was likely the individual who brought the team together, around the vision, in the first place. Consequently, the pastor knows the relative strengths and weaknesses of each team member and, understanding the work the captain must do, also knows which individual is best skilled to carry out such tasks. In fact, in most cases the pastor has no greater motivation in selecting the captain than to see the team succeed – and therefore has a vested interest in appointing someone who will move the team forward most effectively.

When the team selects its own captain, politics are often at the heart of the selection process. Seeing the captain's position as a feather in one's cap rather than as a means of serving others, the team gets off on the wrong foot right at the start, competing for power and perks rather than cooperating for group performance. The team members probably do not know each other's strengths and weaknesses in the beginning, resulting in a heightened prospect of making an inappropriate choice of captain. In fact, few team members are likely to have a solid grasp on the captain's function and are therefore incapable of intelligently selecting the best team member for the job.

There's another good reason for an outsider to choose the captain: the need for the team to have a captain early in its history and for that person to get off to a fast start. Since the team will take time to develop its own pace and inner equilibrium, having a leader in place to foster that development and to help the team capitalize on what it has learned is invaluable. A captain who can make the most of those early developments will win the loyalty and trust of the team; a captain who is ignorant of that growth or misinterprets the lessons will never gain the team's confidence. Having had some history with each team member, the pastor or staff person are more likely to identify the person who will quickly and accurately absorb the lessons emerging from the initial team experiences. In that way, the capable captain solidifies his/her appointment as appropriate.

Unfortunately, there are numerous churches in which captains are selected by pastors or staff for the wrong reasons – usually to maintain control. By installing a captain who will serve the needs, interests or demands of the person who gave them the position, the selector increases the probability of being able to pull the strings of the puppet captain. This situation, of course, is unhealthy and merely reflects the dysfunctional nature of the church. The unhealthy connection between captain and selector often spawns an unhealthy team and leadership environment.

Signs of A Bad Captain

Naturally, there are many times when a team is saddled with a bad captain, no matter who made the selection. It is not a sign of failure or defeat to recognize a bad choice and select a new leader within the team, although that transition must be handled deftly. How do you know when you have a bad captain? These are some of the telltale signs.

117

▭➤ When there is consistent dissension among team members, the captain is failing to harmonize relationships satisfactorily. Sometimes the captain is busy balancing so many other activities that the griping had gone unnoticed, and a simple, discrete observation about the situation made by the team's coach or supervisor will trigger the appropriate response. If a positive adjustment is not forthcoming, however, the failure to squelch the disunity may result in irreparable damage.

▭➤ Some individuals let the position go to their head or they misinterpret the intended role. A captain who becomes overly controlling, making unilateral decisions and informing the team of those decisions, rather than soliciting their input, is a sure sign of this cancer. When a captain reads the position as the delivery of power, it is best to address that problem quickly. If the issue persists, a more radical response may be required.

▭➤ Listen to how team members and congregants describe a given team. If a team becomes labeled "Bob's team" or "Jane's team," and you are able to trace the source of that label to Captain Bob or Captain Jane, then the captain has a misplaced understanding of his/her role. Naturally, in some situations outsiders will designate the team by the name of its most public or competent member, or perhaps by the name of its titular captain. More often, though, this problem stems from the behavior of the captain. When that individual fosters such an identity, or persists in taking credit for what the team has done, this form of personification is unwarranted and unacceptable.

▭➤ In some instances a team begins to focus on its achievements rather than on its vision. Since one of the dominant roles of the captain is to keep members focused on the vision, and to measure all achievements in light of the fulfillment of that vision, this weakness could well be a sign that the captain is ineffective or ill-informed regarding his/her role.

⇨ Great teams solve problems through creativity. If you study the output of a team and notice that its solutions are predictable, uninspired or only moderately successful, the captain may be the culprit. A great captain will not allow the team to accept the path of least resistance; a lazy or incompetent captain may not know the difference, or think it matters.

⇨ Teams that change lives are those that are on the lookout for new opportunities to bring people closer to God and to enhance their life in Christ. That means the team is continually anticipating new options, rather than waiting to respond to existing challenges. A team that is reactive may lack inspired leadership from its captain.

⇨ Talk to team members about how much they enjoy serving on their leadership team. If they exude enthusiasm and joy, the chances are good that their team captain has facilitated a positive leadership environment and is providing stellar support to each member. If the team members are dragging or seem duty-bound rather than ecstatic, the captain is probably letting them down in terms of motivation and focus. Explore what the captain is doing to keep people's spirits high and their sense of impact fed. A captain that does not reinforce the efforts of his team-mates is undermining their ability to persevere and to find the satisfaction that leaders ought to receive from their efforts.

⇨ Do team members complain of the duplication of efforts? That may reflect lack of trust, inferior communication, bad planning, or a lousy captain. Don't jump too quickly to the conclusion that the captain is at fault: sometimes the team will assign internal administrative tasks (e.g., which team member is responsible for a specific task, or evaluating the efficiency with which specific efforts are completed) to one of its members who ordinarily performs such tasks well. In such a case, the problem is that the captain is ineffectively informing that member of sloppy and wasteful work.

⇨ Sometimes captains are in over their heads. This short-changes the captain's position by minimizing the teams processing time in favor of individual productivity. A common result is that everyone on the team works hard and produces individually, but the synergy is absent and the sense of camaraderie that defines true teams is missing.

The existence of one or two of these deficiencies does not necessarily mean that your captain is detrimental to the team. Every leader has his/her weaknesses; the value of the team process is that such deficiencies may be compensated for by the complementary skills of team members. In the same way, every team captain is human and possesses a variety of weaknesses, some more glaring and significant than others. A captain is not automatically disqualified by his/her imperfections: if they were, then we would be stymied once again by the leader-as-superhero problem that team leadership solves. It is only when a captain's weaknesses significantly cripple or disable the team that it may be time to consider a change of internal leadership.

Changing Captains in Midstream

When a change in the captain is merited, the switch is usually called for and carried out by the team itself. While I witnessed a few circumstances in which the pastor or staff made the call, it is usually a sign of a healthy and growing team if it can recognize its own weakness and make the appropriate changes to restore or improve its standing.

Perhaps the most significant aspect related to transitioning the captain is to ensure that the individual who is being relieved of that position is not crushed in the process. In some cases, the departing captain will be reassigned to another team, but unless the person's original passion for the vision that the team is pursuing has changed dramatically, this is a difficult change to justify. More commonly, the captain will simply return to the primary leadership role within the team that he/she originally had, in alignment with his/her leadership aptitude.

The team's coach (usually the pastor or staff liaison) may want to privately but strongly encourage each member to provide immediate acceptance of the new captain along with genuine acceptance of the replaced captain in his/her original role as non-captain team member. Making too big a fuss over the transition makes the change harder; ignoring the transition makes relations on the team awkward. Finding the right balance will be enhanced by the team's coach reminding each member to be honest, sensitive and supportive toward the demoted captain, but to downplay the significance of the transition in favor of focusing even more intently upon the current challenges and opportunities facing the team.

CHAPTER EIGHT

TRANSITIONING TO A TEAM-LED MINISTRY

During the course of scouring the nation for examples of churches that effectively use lay leadership teams, it became obvious that this approach to leadership is the exception to the rule. Even a large majority of the four out of ten churches that claim to be using leadership teams actually have work groups led by an individual leader.

Churches often confuse the notion of teams of leaders working together with the practice of having teams of gifted people serving under the direction of a gifted leader.

One implication is that if churches are going to move toward lay leadership teams, they will be making a dramatic transition from solo-based leadership to team-based leadership. That transition will tax the patience, resources and will of the church. In the end, if the process is properly carried out, the change will justify the effort. But effectively making the shift demands a real commitment to lay-driven ministry, the releasing of leaders to truly lead, the redefining of the role of the pastor and staff, and the recognition and deployment of people's spiritual gifts and natural talents.

123

Let's discuss what it would take for a typical church to make the transition to being led by teams of lay leaders.

Who Leads the Change?

The initial impetus for a move to laity-based team leadership can come from anyone in the church, from the senior pastor to the newest member of the congregation. In effective churches, good ideas come from a wide spectrum of people and places, and the leaders of the church are wise enough and sufficiently open to consider those that have potential.

Once the idea of lay-team leadership is on the table, it is difficult to make the transition unless the Senior Pastor is supportive. The transition will redefine his/her role and will require that the pastor facilitate the switch to new ways of allocating power, distributing responsibility and resources, communicating with the congregation, and evaluating ministry outcomes. While it is theoretically possible for a church to make the transition in spite of the indifference or opposition of the Senior Pastor, that is likely to happen only if that pastor has very limited influence in the church's decision-making process, and if he/she is not looked to by the congregation for behavioral and procedural cues. In most churches, even though the influence of the Senior Pastor is not what it used to be, the pastor remains the dominant agent of influence concerning the nature and direction of the church.

There is a difference between identifying the primary change agent and ensuring that key influencers within the congregation and on staff support the proposed change. There are many examples of churches where the pastor was ready to make the switch from solo leadership to team leadership, but was ineffective at building the supportive coalition required to facilitate the move. In African-American churches, what the pastor says is usually accepted without question: black congregations more readily accept moving from solo leadership to team leadership, if the pastor promotes the shift. In Caucasian churches, though, a change of this magnitude may not even get a fair hearing within the congregation, no matter what the pastor desires. If the idea is proposed, backed by the Senior Pastor, and finds initial favor among the people, then the key to success is whether or not the people trust their leaders to make good decisions, and how effective those leaders are at mobilizing people around the details and implications of the transition.

In most churches, the scenario that has worked well begins with the Senior Pastor embracing the idea, regardless of where the idea came from or who introduced the possibility. How the pastor handles the idea, though, will likely determine the fate of lay leadership teams at the church.

If the church has a Senior Pastor working in conjunction with other ministry staff, then the pastor may fruitfully initiate the transition by building a strong team at the professional staff level. This is important because it sends the message to the congregation and staff that the pastor is both serious about integrating this process into the life of the church and that he/she is skilled at facilitating that reality. Because people learn best by watching a model in action, providing the congregation with a working example of how teams operate and the benefit they bring to the ministry is a powerful and valuable step in sparking the transition. If the church is small and has only the Senior Pastor as its professional ministry personnel, then the pastor must focus on treating core lay leaders as the people who will become the practical advocates of team-based lay leadership.

Whether the church is large or small, the pastor must become a champion of the change to all who might be influenced by it. In addition to modeling teamwork and encouraging people to minister with a team mentality, this means that the pastor must strategically initiate the transition. Among the tasks he/she must integrate are preparing the congregation – intellectually, theologically, operationally and emotionally – to make the change. This implies teaching about leadership and churchmanship from a team-driven perspective; repositioning people's notions of power, authority, responsibility and influence; and getting people used to the notion of the pastor no longer being the primary leader of everything in the church, but providing strategic leadership to core leaders.

People respond well to changes that promise greater value and benefit than sacrifice and suffering. But a constant in all leadership experience is that most people resist change, even when it is in their personal best interests. Jack Welch, the former CEO of General Electric, once brilliantly observed, "Change has no constituency." If you plan to make the change to team-based leadership, get ready for a fight. The breadth and intensity of the battle depends upon how well you prepare people for the shift, in advance of initiating the transition, and how strategic you have been in aligning key leaders to support the move prior to "going public" with the idea.

Changing the Church Culture

Once the idea has been floated publicly, a series of foundations have to be put in place to increase the chances of having a successful transition. The first and most far-reaching of those changes relates to the culture of the church.

Every church has a culture – the system of meaning and the ministry context that defines your church. A culture is the cumulative body of symbols, traditions, values, acceptable behaviors, ideals, language, and customs that create a unified way of life and a unique means of interpreting and experiencing reality. Your church's culture affects everything related to the ministry. If you want the transition to lay-led leadership teams, you must align the church's culture with the requirements and practices found in the team-based approach.

The shift in culture may entail a variety of new perspectives that congregants should adopt. For instance, one useful shift would be altering the notion of leaders as volunteers to leaders as lay ministers. Along with such a change in perception and terminology would come a transition in the treatment of lay ministers, moving from status as unpaid laborers to that of part-time ministry professionals still unpaid, but regarded as equals in ministry. Repositioning various perspectives will facilitate the move from solo to team leadership.

In addition, our observations suggest that the transition will fail unless a church's values are consistent with a team-based approach. Values are the principles and standards that define what is right, desirable and worthwhile within the system in question. Your values therefore delineate your character as a ministry. But be aware that there are two types of values that churches possess: stated and latent. In the past decade it has become common for churches to fashion a "values statement" that defines the values of the church. Common elements in those statements include items such as integrity, personal holiness, humility, confession, servanthood, and so forth. Just as powerful and significant, though, are the latent values – that is, the values that are not written in an official church document but are observable in the accepted or expected behavior and thinking of the church. Healthy congregations purposefully align their stated and latent values; when these are disjointed, politics replaces faith as the dominant focus of the church.

If you want to move to team-based leadership, then your values must promote such an environment and practice. Here are some of the items you might consider integrating into both your stated and latent core values, if these are not already part of your core corporate values.

1. The church promotes the identification and application of <u>personal spiritual gifts</u>, used for the good of the worldwide Church, the benefit of the local body of believers, and the joy and fulfillment of the individual in service to the Kingdom of God (1 Cor. 12:4-8).

2. All of the church's ministry efforts are geared toward <u>promoting God's kingdom</u>, not individual agendas or splinter group priorities (Matt 6:33).

127

3. All work that is done by the church is to be done with excellence, with the realization that we are working for God, not for men or institutions (Col 3:23).

4. The body of Christ is best served by collaboration, not competition. Whenever possible, congregants will work together toward a common outcome, rather than vie for resources and commendations based on individual productivity (Matt. 20:20-28).

5. The Church reflects the unity of God when its leaders work in close-knit cooperation toward a commonly held vision from the Lord. Rather than seek leadership from individuals of extraordinary ability, this church strives to build teams of God-gifted believers combining their unique and complementary abilities toward the fulfillment of that vision. Teamwork focused on following God's will for the church is always supported more readily than isolated individual efforts (Acts 6:1-6).

6. The health of this ministry is witnessed by reliance upon multiple leaders rather than upon the direction provided by a single leader. While the church esteems the Senior Pastor as the individual whom God has ordained to provide the ultimate direction to His people, the pastor succeeds by empowering the other leaders God has brought to the congregation to use their gifts and abilities in service to God and to the body of believers (Acts 15:1-22).

7. This ministry is to be evaluated not only according to what it does, but also according to how it ministers; in addition to the results we produce, we will also be judged by the processes through which those outcomes are achieved. The church does not accept the notion that God's vision will be pursued and fulfilled by the congregation "at any cost" since there are various methods, behaviors and perspectives that may lead to desired results through reliance upon inappropriate means (Rev. 3:1-3).

Your church's values charter may include a large number of values or a brief recitation of principles and standards. Regardless of the quantity involved, specifying those elements and making them clearly known through teaching and application, is vital to the transition.

Nailing the Details

Another key procedure in the early stages of the transition is for the transition team – i.e., the Senior Pastor along with his/her confidantes in bringing about this shift – to make sure that everyone has a clear and identical understanding of what is being contemplated and implemented.

One aspect of this unification process requires the clarification of language used in the transition. Terms commonly thrown about must be carefully defined and those definitions widely disseminated. Among the terms that ought to be clearly understood and embraced are those described in chapter 2: leadership, team leadership, work groups, values, goals, vision, healthy ministry, and successful ministry. There is often value generated by addressing the roles of key players whose lives will be affected in this transition, such as the Senior Pastor, elders, deacons, committee chairpersons, and church staff.

Another set of helpful clarifications relate to key distinctions that will further people's understanding of the changes under consideration. For instance, do people know the difference between spiritual gifts and natural talents, and the significance of each? Do they understand the different leadership aptitudes and how they best fit together? Is there a clear comprehension of the difference between trying hard and accomplishing good outcomes? Are congregants wise to the distinction between process and product, and the implications related to these divergent but closely related elements?

In the early stage of the transition process, it is advisable to delineate the specific components of the team design that the church hopes to embrace. This means outlining details such as the ideal number of people to be incorporated into leadership teams; the specific roles that leaders will play within those teams (e.g., Directing, Strategic, Team-Building, and Operational, or some other useful designations); the specific elements to be included in each team's charter or covenant; the process by which team members will be selected and invited onto a team; the dynamics of the lay leader-pastor-staff relationships; and the role of apprenticeships in the process.

A Plan of Action

Once the idea of moving to lay leadership teams has been embraced by the primary change agent (usually the Senior Pastor) and the church's culture and the transitional details have been addressed, then a specific transition plan must be developed. There is no standard formula for doing this. However, certain elements seem to be generally involved in the action plan.

One of the most strategic decisions is to start small, iron out the miscues in the process, expand slowly, and eventually complete the transition with limited public fanfare. This low-key approach not only minimizes initial resistance, but also builds congregational confidence in the process and in the team concept. Once there are a handful of lay-leader teams working smoothly and generating positive results, the congregation is likely to jump on the bandwagon: we may be living in an age of sophistication, but the old axiom "everybody loves a winner" remains as relevant today as ever.

This intimates that the initial team you select must be your best prospect for achieving success through team ministry. This team will be your experimental group and will have to endure hardships and challenges that succeeding teams will not have to bear. The underlying notion is that if this, your best team, cannot make it, then there are other serious problems that need to be solved before the process is integrated throughout the church's ministry.

In the action plan for the transition, be sure to allow sufficient time for the experiment to produce as many insights as possible that will lead to a successful changeover. In some circumstances, speed is essential to success; when transitioning from solo-based leadership to team-based leadership, though, speed can be deadly. There is a slow learning curve that must be exploited to its fullest extent if the aggregate shift is to reap long-term benefits. Keep in mind that this is not just a change in the contours of leadership, but a redefinition of the very culture of the church. Allow for the time that such a grand transformation deserves.

Once the initial team has solidified and begun to operate efficiently, effectively and consistently, use that initial triumph as a case study to persuade the skeptics in the congregation that the process is viable. It is best to be upfront about the lessons learned in the process and to describe how those hard-won insights will be incorporated into the development of additional teams at the church.

In the action plan, be sure to identify the foundational teams that the church will strive to create. This means differentiating between the macro-level and micro-level leadership teams to be created. Macro-level teams are those that lead the aggregate ministry of the church. In most cases, there will be one macro-level team that will likely consist of a combination of several vocational and avocational individuals (e.g., the Senior Pastor, a staff person and two elders) whose combined gifts enable them to strategically lead the church. Every church is likely to have a variety of micro-level teams – groups of leaders who share the responsibility for directing the specific ministries within the church. For instance, there might be a leadership team for worship, one for evangelism, another for discipleship, one for stewardship, a team focused on community, and yet another to lead in the area of community service ministry.[1] (Keep in mind that the leadership team is not necessarily the individuals who will do the upfront work in that ministry – e.g., "worship leaders" who will play instruments and sing in the worship service. They are the individuals who conceptualize, orchestrate, resource, facilitate and evaluate the implementation of the music in the worship service.)

The macro-level leadership team will maintain the broadest view of the church's ministry, focusing upon the aggregate ministry efforts of the church and how those efforts relate to the church's vision. That team is responsible for keeping other teams, as well as congregants, focused on the grand vision of the church. In contrast, each of the micro-level teams must be intimately acquainted with the church's overall vision, and how their area of ministry relates to that vision, but will be most passionately pursuing the component of the vision for which their team is primarily responsible.

The action plan may encompass the identification of the micro-level teams; a schedule for the introduction of each team into the life of the church; the training and developmental resources required to facilitate the team leadership rollout; the means of identifying potential leaders; the leaders and management process by which the team rollout will be driven; the transition from existing leadership groups (e.g., elders, deacons) to leadership teams; the methods to be used for resolving disputes that arise from the transition; and how to handle questions that arise within the congregation about the transition. The action plan might also include information about how this entire process will be communicated to the congregation; how people who are not leaders will be integrated into the flow of ministry under the new approach; and an outline describing how leadership teams will interact with each other to coordinate the aggregate ministry of the church.

Internal Accountability

The success of the process will ultimately depend upon how well the church prepares teams and team members to integrate a realistic accountability method into the leadership framework. Excellence only occurs when there are standards that are known and applied. Most people will live up to the expectations placed upon them if they believe that they will be held accountable for their performance. The same principle seems to hold true for teams: comprised of human beings, they will do as little as they have to in order to get by, but they will do whatever is necessary to avoid failing or to live up to the expectations they have agreed to uphold.

What should you hold leaders accountable for? Every leader is qualified to lead because God has called him/her to that task (and has therefore gifted them for it) and because they have exhibited biblical character. There is a high probability that the calling will not change; as long as we seek to fulfill that calling, we have little to worry about on this score. This means that the primary focus for accountability among leaders is in the realm of character: do we consistently and unerringly live in accordance with God's moral standards? A leader may prove to be incompetent and require training to raise his/her performance capacity, but that does not disqualify them from serving in leadership. Breaking God's moral code, however, represents a serious breach of trust and responsibility and may qualify as grounds for dismissal from the ranks of the church's leaders.

Leadership competencies – the functions that leaders under-take to motivate, mobilize, resource and direct God's people in pursuit of His vision – are another area for which leaders should be held accountable. The purpose of this evaluative emphasis, however, is not so much to prove or disprove the worthiness of someone to lead as it is to identify the strengths and weaknesses of the leader so that he/she may improve their levels of skill and leadership performance.

Leaders are responsible for facilitating ministry outcomes, so there must also be a degree of accountability for the results that were produced under the leadership of each individual team. While many will argue that God's greatest concern is certainly with who we are rather than what we achieve, one of the distinctives of leaders is that they serve in order to facilitate life transformation within the body of believers. If such life transformation is not occurring, then we must question their capacity to lead. At the very least, the failure to produce positive spiritual outcomes identifies aspects of development that would enhance the individual's leadership.

Team leadership also requires some assessment of the quality of community that has been fostered within each leadership collective. The team-driven approach requires different skills, perspectives and measures than are relevant to solo-based leadership. One of the keys to successful teamwork is the nature and depth of the relationships developed among team members. Examining the strength of the community that has emerged within the team is a telltale sign of the maturity and potential of the team.

What Happens If Some Teams Fail ?

Sometimes even the most strategic and well-planned changes do not work out as planned. What happens if one (or more) of the lay leadership teams fail?

To address that question, first we have to define what it means for a team to fail. There are seven chief ways in which any team might fail. Your church should have a clear strategy of how it intends to handle each type of failure, should any of these occur. Let's look at each possibility and determine what might be done in response to such failure.

First, a team could deteriorate due to the moral failure of one or more of its members. Experience shows that it is uncommon for multiple team members to experience moral failure simultaneously; usually, one member fails to live up to God's moral standards. The response to moral failure depends upon the culture of the church. Some churches believe that part of being in community is restoring a fallen member; others contend that because of the position of leaders, moral failure immediately disqualifies the individual from further leadership participation. In either case, you must also determine at what point a fallen leader is qualified to return to leadership responsibility.

Second, a team fails in its function if it reverts to solo leadership practices. This defeats the reason for developing the team framework in the first place and undermines the investment of trust and resources in team members and the team process. The church must determine if the failure is systemic or related to the individuals in the team. The solution could be as simple as providing better definitions of team leadership or as dramatic as disbanding the team and replacing it with a new collection of leaders who are passionate about the same vision that had drawn the original team together.

A third way teams fail is when they fail to provide the initiative in ministry. Teams that wait for someone to point them in the right direction, to tell them what to do, to identify existing problems or opportunities are of little use to the church. This is particularly true since a team-based ministry demands cross-team integration – i.e., multiple teams, each focused on a different dimension of the macro-level vision, working cooperatively. Often, working with the Directing Leader in the unit stimulates an appropriate improvement, since this person is largely responsible for motivating the group to stay excited about and focused upon their vision, and to aggressively seek options for action.

The fourth common letdown is when the team fails to motivate the congregation to understand, own, and actively participate in the pursuit of the vision. If leaders, who are the primary champions of the vision, cannot get others excited about the vision, who will? Sometimes the failure is because the team members are so enthusiastic about the possibilities that they take on the task of fulfilling the vision without encompassing the efforts of outsiders. Other times the motivational skills of team members are not sufficient to generate congregational excitement and involvement. No matter what the underlying deficiency might be, getting the congregation to invest themselves in the totality of the ministry is imperative.

Sometimes the issue at stake is the inability to mobilize people around specific tasks in order to facilitate desired outcomes. While this may seem like a simple management function, the inability to organize people appropriately can dampen their enthusiasm for investing in the process. Occasionally you may find that the problem is miscommunication within the team (e.g., the Directing Leader assumed the Team-Building Leader would handle it, the Team-Building Leader perceived this to be the job of the Operational Leader, and so forth). In other instances, the issue is deeper: the leaders failed to think through how to efficiently identify and utilize the talents of the laity who demonstrated an interest in helping the team.

A sixth example of failure is attributable to not delivering the promised results. Leaders exist to serve people by helping them to achieve specific outcomes, as described by the team's vision. Whether the failure can be traced to a misunderstanding of the vision, a lack of adequate planning to generate desirable outcomes, the acceptance of inappropriate goals, or some other shortcoming, teams that do not produce results provide limited value to the ministry. People are leaders because they have the ability to identify specific outcomes and to produce those results. When leaders do not produce, they not only fail themselves and their team, but they let down the entire ministry they were called to serve. If that sounds harsh or overstated – many pastors protest when I describe this situation as evidence that leaders have failed – then you do not understand the responsibility that leaders shoulder when they accept their calling to lead. Merely trying hard or "doing your best" does not constitute effective leadership; it is provided by doing what-ever it takes, within the boundaries of God's standards and people's capabilities, to deliver the results that do justice to the vision and honor His calling to His Church.

The final instance of failure is when a team leaves God out of the process. Effective teams pray constantly, and always seek the Lord's wisdom prior to any decisions they make. God's leaders always consider His principles and standards before moving ahead. The best leadership teams engage in serious spiritual development so that they have a deep and compelling relationship with the Lord whom they serve as leaders. Great teams always give the Lord the credit for the incredible things that happen as a result of their hard work and diligent efforts. If a team fails to integrate the ways of the Lord into their work, they become a business enterprise, using their abilities and resources to foster positive results. God expects more of His leaders than that – and anything less than a complete integration of God into the process and product of the team can be interpreted as failure.

Most lay leadership teams experience failure throughout their life cycle. However, such failure need not be permanent, nor must it be debilitating. Great teams recognize their failings and use them as a springboard to success. Failure is one of the great teachers in life, if we treat those failures as God's way of waking us up to our fullest potential. The church may wish to introduce ways of sensitizing its teams to their own failures, either through the accountability process, the training process or other means. Be prepared to identify team failures and to nurture members in appropriate ways through those defeats.

When Is the Change Complete?

Be prepared for the transition to take a substantial amount of time – perhaps as long as two or three years. If this seems excessive, consider all that goes into the transition: redefining the role of the pastor (and staff), altering the culture of the ministry, motivating the congregation to change its roles and expectations, transitioning existing power and authority relationships, revising the lines of communication, elevating the importance of spiritual gifts and the ministry vision, and developing and implementing an entirely divergent evaluation procedure. In essence, you are reinventing your ministry. That's not going to happen overnight.

You might find that the healthier your church is, the more resistance you get from people who cling to the "if it ain't broke, don't fix it" philosophy. If your church is more than 50 years old, you are likely to meet resistance based upon the history of the church – the infamous "we've never done it that way before" mentality. If you have a relatively small contingent of powerbrokers in the body – the founding families, the major donors, the political sharks – then you may experience political maneuvering that would do the Democratic and Republican Parties proud.

If you are a leader in your church and you can see the incredible potential of using a team-based approach to carrying out the vision, do not become dejected by the reluctance or outright opposition of so many congregants who are otherwise sane, intelligent and savvy. Change is always painful for some, and it always comes with a price tag attached. Pray hard about the feasibility of converting to lay leadership teams. When you are persuaded that the Lord will be honored by the change, prepare for the conflict that the shift will unleash, and strategically present the possibilities to those who can facilitate a smooth transition. Perhaps, as several churches did, you will want to demonstrate the power of teams by appointing a team to facilitate the transition itself!

The transition will be completed when more than two-thirds of your active congregants expect all leadership provided within the church to be accomplished by teams, rather than by solo practitioners, and when more than 80% of the leadership provided is actually delivered by teams rather than individuals. At that stage realize that the momentum has swung in favor of teams, and the future of leadership in your church is not likely to revert to solo leadership without a concerted and overt effort to go backwards in time. When you have reached the point of team dominance, mark it with a celebration – not because you succeeded in establishing a major transition – but because the existence of team-based leadership and a congregation that esteems teams reflects another plateau of health achieved by your church.

FOOTNOTES

[1] You may notice that what I have suggested is lay leadership teams focused around the six pillars of the church, as described in Acts as well as in my previous book, The Habits of Highly Effective Churches. To facilitate effective leadership teams, build them around the basic foundations of your church's ministry how ever you choose to organize it. Each "department" or "division" of the ministry should interact with its own focused team. For more insight into the notion of organizing around the six pillars, see *The Habits of Highly Effective Churches*, George Barna, Regal Books, Ventura, CA, 2000.

CHAPTER NINE

LANDMINES IN
TEAM TERRITORY

No matter how carefully you plan your transition to a team-based leadership approach, you will undoubtedly experience significant challenges along the way. Based on our exploration of the process that many team-based churches have undertaken, allow me to identify some of those landmines that are awaiting your arrival. The types of challenges might be categorized as those related to providing consistency in leadership; the appropriate allocation of leadership and ministry resources; introducing and maintaining appropriate processes for team leadership; and handling people's expectations. Be forewarned and prepare an intelligent response to these possible dangers.

Challenges Related to Consistency in Leadership

Leaders are people who take risks, but the nature of the leadership they provide must have a high degree of predictability and consistency if followers are to remain confident in, and devoted to, their leaders. Consider some of the difficulties leaders will face regarding the ability to provide consistent leadership.

Lacking the Motivation

When you were young, you probably believed that your parents never got tired of being a parent and that they needed no encouragement to continue in that role. It may have seemed as if their only purpose for being on earth was to be your mother or father, and that no amount of positive reinforcement would alter their commitment to, or fulfillment derived from, that task.

Christians tend to treat church leaders the same way as kids treat their parents: we assume that church leaders get such immeasurable pleasure and satisfaction from the practice of leading that they need no applause or commendations. How wrong that sentiment is! Even though leading is sometimes an enjoyable function for those who are called to it, it can also be a taxing and thankless task. Being human, leaders need to receive occasional indications that their efforts are significant and producing worthwhile results. Because a church's lay leaders do not receive any financial remuneration for their efforts, the compensation they derive is psychological and emotional. How can you facilitate such support for their efforts?

First, help them to remain focused on the vision of their team. The vision was the outcome that initially sparked their passion and motivated them to dive into the fray. If a leader truly grasps God's vision for his/her life and ministry, understands how it connects with the vision of the team, and how the pursuit of that vision will bolster the impact and wholeness of the church, the chances of them ignoring the opportunity to serve through the team or of becoming blasé about God's vision are minimal. Leaders are vision-driven people. Keeping them focused on the incredible influence of God's vision stokes a true leader's passion to deliver whatever it takes to bring that potential to reality.

Second, a few words and gestures of sincere appreciation and encouragement go a long way toward restoring the energy and commitment of leaders. While a great leader does not live for personal compliments and external rewards, all human beings are moved by kind words and tangible expressions of gratitude. What can you do to stimulate your congregation to develop the habit of passing on a genuine vote of confidence or a heartfelt expression of thanks for the life-changing labor of the church's leaders? Rather than taking leaders for granted, what can be done to build a church-wide culture that esteems and affirms its leaders on a regular basis?

Third, have you created mechanisms that allow leaders to come in contact with individuals whose lives have been changed by the work of the leader's team? Personal testimonies of impact lift the spirits of leaders faster than anything else I've seen. A collection of testimonies may not represent a valid assessment of the impact and quality of a team's ministry, but stories of life change often make leaders feel that the time and effort they have sacrificed on behalf of the ministry – time spent away from family, time drawn from leisure, time devoted to ministry after long, hard days at their job – is paying off in eternal dividends.

Finally, there is value to pointing each leader back toward the initial reason for their involvement on the team: the sense that God called them to lead, and that their leadership is a central facet of their personal service to Jesus Christ. Once God's calling is clear, what else would you do? What other endeavor could possibly bring resonant, lasting fulfillment to a leader than to fulfill that calling? Discouragement and fatigue are enemies of every leader. During times of despair, discouragement and fatigue, a leader may wistfully dream about other ministry opportunities. Sometimes it is helpful to play out a scenario of the "greener pasture" to underscore how unfulfilling such a transition would become. We draw our greatest satisfaction from those things to which God has called us; sometimes we need to be reminded of that principle.

Burning Out Your People

What happens in your ministry when you find a good leader? In many churches, that individual is used as broadly and as often as possible. "Good leaders are hard to find. When I find one, I use him wherever he can be useful," admitted one pastor we interviewed. Doesn't that create problems, such as burnout, being spread too thin, lacking deep passion for the ministries in which he gets involved? "Yeah, I suppose so, but we need help. I can't worry about him being burned out tomorrow when I've got fires to put out today. If I have a leader, what choice do I have but to use him where he's needed, when he's needed?"

141

There is the danger that the same philosophy – essentially using the leader as a jack-of-all-trades troubleshooter – will be adopted in a team leadership environment. In practical terms, you might be tempted to allow, or even encourage, your best leaders to serve on two or three teams simultaneously, or to move them from place to place to patch holes or shake up dormant teams.

Take a tip from the churches that have perfected the art of lay leadership teams: limit each leader to one team at a time, and let them focus on the team whose vision released their passion. Such a limitation may produce temporary hardships while you search for additional leaders to join nascent or rebuilt teams, but the long-term benefits justify the short-term pain. The leader will last longer, thus enhancing the value of the team on which he/she serves – and increasing the benefit to the church. The leader will be more effective and add greater value to the ministry by being able to focus all of his/her energy and abilities on the challenges facing one team, rather than suffering from distraction and divided loyalties by serving on multiple teams simultaneously. The individual is also likely to appreciate the opportunity to invest fully in the vision that stokes his/her passion, rather than simply serving on two or more teams where natural skills and past experiences make them a solid if uninspired contributor.

Don't be surprised if you encounter a few leaders who ask to serve on two or more teams at the same time. Many capable leaders are energetic, impatient, self-confident, and more than a few also savor the prospect of being able to "save" failing ministries. Be sure that someone in the ministry has a clear understanding of the importance of saying "no" to requests to serve in multiple capacities at once, and has the authority to enforce that policy. No matter how silly such a rule may seem at the outset, years of experience in team-led churches across the nation have verified the value of helping the most aggressive of lay leaders to narrow their sights and channel their capacity to the productivity of one team.

Replacing Lost Leaders

One of the joys of a successful lay leadership program is watching teams take the church to the next level of ministry impact. One of the most disappointing experiences is watching a great team lose a key member. The reasons for such losses run the gamut from the unpredictable (death or illness, job relocation) to the disheartening (moral failure, divorce) to the foolish (burnout). Turnover is unavoidable. How your church handles these situations will determine the ultimate viability of the team.

Regardless of the reason for the departure of a valued member, the team must be allowed to grieve the loss. That process requires time, some internal "space," and emotional sensitivity. The more closely-knit the team becomes, the more like a family it behaves. Just as a family would have to work through the impact of losing one of its members, so must a healthy team invest significant time and energy in addressing the emotional, spiritual, intellectual and productivity implications of the loss.

Most teams will choose to continue despite the transition – and rightly so. Because teams do not hinge on the presence or absence of a single individual, it is more plausible to replace a team member who is removed from the leadership mix than to replace a high-profile solo leader who leaves the scene. There will be a time of adjustment necessary as the team integrates a new leader to replace the departed colleague. Although the team will rely upon the relationships and other internal strengths that have been built up over time, it will take intentional effort and dedicated time to redefine the team's nature and relationships with the new, incoming partner.

If the church has followed the pattern of other churches that have successfully intertwined teams into their ministry, they will have an apprentice available to assist the affected team. While that person is not likely to be a carbon copy of the lost member, moving the departed leader's apprentice into the team's open slot will smooth the transition. The team may handle the presence of the apprentice in various ways, such as treating his/her assistance as a temporary fix until a more permanent replacement can be identified and invited, or "trying out" the apprentice as a potential permanent replacement. Either way, the apprentice should enable the team to continue to provide effective leadership until a strategic determination about the team's direction is made.

Disbanding the Successful Team

Sometimes the best advice is counter-intuitive. An example of such counsel is to disband a team that has successfully fulfilled its vision.

Why would a church voluntarily break up a unit that has proven its capacity to serve effectively? The heart of the issue relates to the purpose for the team's existence – namely, to fulfill the vision. The vision is what attracted these individuals to that particular team. The vision is what ignited their passion. Once the vision has been brought to reality, the team may no longer have a reason to exist.

It is difficult for organizations to accept the idea that every relationship has a definable life cycle. A team created for the purpose of accomplishing a specified outcome loses its reason for being once that outcome has come to fruition. Disbanding that team is not an admission of failure, but a sign of the ministry's maturity.

Would assigning the team to a new vision or allowing it to create a new role for itself better serve the ministry? The answer is usually "no." The best strategy is to celebrate the success of the team, officially dissolve the collective, and encourage each of them to discern God's next direction for them to pursue. Being released to follow his/her new ministry passion will enable each team member to maximize the benefit delivered to the church. Insisting that the team hang on beyond its time would undermine the vitality and impact of the group. Acknowledging the value that the team has provided, while helping each individual to get a fresh start on a new team will keep each leader invigorated and productive.

Realistically, God's vision for a church or a team is not something that is accomplished quickly. The vision usually takes years of concentrated, faithful effort before it becomes a reality. In many cases, a team will be together for a decade or more. Sometimes, the vision outlives the team. However, when the team has reached the top of its mountain, it may choose to search the landscape for new challenges to pursue, or it may sense a need to stay together to build on the vision that it has helped to bring to reality.

When the Transitioning Pastor Transitions Out

Leading a church from solo leadership to team leadership takes time, a comprehensive process, congregational trust in its leaders, a commitment to making teams successful and a transitional leader. The transitional leader is sometimes a gifted layperson, pastoral associate or staff person, but is often the senior pastor. Facilitating the shift to team leadership may well be the crowning organizational achievement of the pastor's ministry career.

However, for that transition to be successful, the pastor must be at the church long enough to complete the transition and to nurture it through its first year or two after the change has been implemented. Some denominations regularly move pastors from one church to another, and moving a pastor who is in the midst of a transition process could cripple the church for many years to come by removing the process champion in midstream. In other cases, although this has been rare, the senior pastor decides to retire or change pastorates in the midst of the transition. In still other instances, the church gets immersed in the transition and then changes its mind, and effectively closes down the process by firing its pastor. Any of these situations will severely harm the church.

If you serve a denomination that reassigns pastors to churches, covenant with the denomination to remain at the church undergoing the transition until it is completed. If the denomination is not willing to make such an agreement, you have two alternatives: develop a layperson to spearhead the shift, or avoid the transition until there will be sufficient leadership stability to complete the transaction.

If you are a pastor who would be the primary leader of a move to teams, but you are not totally committed to being at your church for the next four or five years, lay the foundation for your successor to make the shift. One of your greatest parting gifts to the congregation will be to prepare them for the transition without initiating it prematurely.

If you are the pastor who will spearhead a shift to teams, be sure to acquire the support of key influencers within the congregation prior to instigating the change. There will undoubtedly be a few laypersons whose sense of power, authority and prominence will be undermined by the shift. Work with your base of supporters to ensure that threatened or potentially disgruntled individuals do not hinder what is best for the church.

Allocation of Resources

One of the danger zones relates to allocating resources. There is a natural tendency for people – and, especially, for leaders – to desire more authority, more power, more budget, more people, more responsibility, more of just about everything. How ministry resources get allocated can produce astounding breakthroughs – or shatter the strength and focus of teams, bringing the ministry down with them. Here are several potential hot potatoes related to the allocation of resources.

Driving the Communications Process

Some churches expect their lay leaders to drive the communications process that exists between the pastor/staff and leadership team. "We're fulltime ministry professionals," explained one pastor at a church that was struggling with its team process. "If the team wants information or other resources, they know where to find us. We are very comfortable waiting for them to initiate contact."

A more sensible and fruitful strategy is to expect the ministry professionals to direct the communications flow with each of the church's leadership teams. Although some people might see things differently, the most reasonable perspective is to acknowledge that the pastor and staff (if the church has ministry staff) exist to serve the ministry efforts of the laity. Thousands of churches are suffering today because they have the nature of that relationship backwards, expecting the laity to do whatever they can to facilitate the ministry of the paid professionals. The ideal situation is a positive, intimate, symbiotic relationship between the clergy and laity, but when push comes to shove, the clergy are on the payroll to foster the efforts of the congregation.

As employees of the ministry, the pastor and staff likely have an easier time of accessing information and resources that will help each leadership team do its job most effectively. Consequently, it makes sense for the pastor and staff to take the initiative to stay in touch with the team, to divulge information that would help them, to facilitate the provision of existing resources for the their work, and to regularly debrief the team to determine how the church might best support their future efforts. Expecting the team to perform this function is inviting disaster.

Stockpiling Talent

Leaders attract leaders, and winners attract everybody. You will undoubtedly face a situation at some point in which one particular team begins to horde leaders. This is the church equivalent of a championship sports team stockpiling talented players who will forfeit their ability to make gobs of money to star on lesser teams in favor of taking less money for the chance to play with a winner. One of your lay teams will likely emerge as a superior blend of talents, no matter how low-key, humble or servant-oriented they may be. Other leaders may strive to get attached to that team, even as an apprentice or "second string" leader, simply for the joy of being where the action is and seeing success after success up close.

147

This spectacle has the potential to destroy all of your teams. First, when leaders run to a team because of its success, they lose sight of the most important motivation for joining one: the team's vision. Second, when one or a handful of teams are allowed to bank talent for future use, the church will suffer in the immediate period by not having access to the leaders that God provided for the present day. Third, the stockpiled leaders will lose the opportunity to experience the joy of serving and growing at an optimal pace. Instead, they will watch others serve while they simmer in the minor leagues. Fourth, the overt envy shown of certain teams will breed jealousy, in-fighting, and other unhealthy attitudes and behaviors.

One of the most intriguing qualities of churches that attract leaders or finds itself blessed with an abundance of such individuals is that they disallow stockpiling in favor of moving unassigned leaders onto new teams, resulting in rampant innovation. You can never have enough leaders and you will never have too many leaders, if you orchestrate their interaction to permit creative partnerships and entrepreneurial activity. You might consider prohibiting putting leadership talent "on ice" as a breach of church values. Allow each team to gather the human resources it needs and direct additional talented individuals to other opportunities within the ministry.

The Team Leadership Development Process

No matter how great an idea team leadership may be, you can count on the transition from solo leadership to team-based leadership stirring significant dissension and controversy. From those who figure to lose some degree of autonomy and power, to those who resist dismantling the way things have always been, to those who simply hate change, prepare yourself for some lively discussions and savvy politicking. Good things never come easy; a shift from solo-based leadership to team-based leadership will prove the point. You may wish to prepare for some of the following barriers to a smooth transition.

Untouchable Teams

During the transition from solo-based leadership to team-based leadership you will undoubtedly run into a few people who suggest that the team process be adopted, but that existing "teams" be "grandfathered" into the new system. In other words, existing groups of individuals who fill a leadership capacity in the church should be exempted from the new rules and fresh approach by virtue of their existence prior to the new systems. The most common groups that request such "untouchable" status are the elders and the deacons.

If you cave in to such demands, you are asking for severe headaches in the near future. As you develop a church culture that proclaims team leadership to be the only acceptable approach to leading the church, permitting pre-existing exceptions undermines your culture and the potential for your teams. Many pastors have argued that their elders and deacons are already serving as a leadership team. In my experience, however, most elders and deacons are not leaders; those groups are too large to operate as an effective team; they are not wed to a common vision that brought them together in the first place; and they do not have complimentary leadership aptitudes that facilitate ministry efficacy. I am not arguing for the elimination of elders and deacons; I am arguing for philosophical and practical consistency in how your church is led. Maintain a board of elders or deacons, but reduce its size to make it a manageable group of true leaders who reflect the demeanor of leadership teams.

At some point in your transition from solo leadership to team leadership you will encounter the conflict with traditions. This may well be the place where you address the role of traditional behavior and thinking: how should the eldership of the church be handled? Typically, you will fight battles concerning the reduction in the number of elders, the revisions in the core criteria for selecting elders, and the very purpose of elders within the church. Rather than a group of individuals who have a significant history at the church and a true affection for it, the elders transition to become the chief leadership council of the church – a small group of leaders who focus on the aggregate ministry and spiritual health of the congregation.

For some churches, that reflects no change at all – but for most congregations, this approach represents a radical and wrenching shift in direction, policy, practice and perspective. If you choose to use teams, be prepared to fight this battle.

Infiltration by the Professionals

In many churches, the rule is that every team must include at least one pastor or staff person, and in some cases I have seen churches require that a pastor or staffer be the team captain. It usually doesn't take too much digging to discover that this is a reflection of the church professionals' desire to maintain control of the ministry and to retain a significant influence over all decisions.

Again, we need to distinguish between macro-level and micro-level teams. At the macro-level – that is, teams that focus on the aggregate ministry of the church, providing comprehensive leadership to the totality of the church – it may be deemed entirely appropriate to invite a pastor onto that team. At the micro-level, however – i.e., teams that lead specific dimensions of the aggregate ministry, such as the worship ministry, the outreach ministry, the Christian education ministry – it is less advisable to incorporate clergy and church professionals onto the teams, unless absolutely necessary to do so.

There are times – particularly in situations of crisis, a small church just beginning a team process or where the pastor or staff person has extraordinary expertise – when assigning a pastor or staff person to a team make perfect sense. Generally speaking, though, populating each ministry team with qualified, passionate lay people is preferable to mixing staff and laity. Pastors and staff may most profitably serve as advisors to one or more teams, and there may be times when the experience and knowledge of those individuals encourages a team to annex that person for a period of time in what amounts to a consulting capacity.

Avoiding the Apprenticeship

Churches that have successful teams incorporate an apprenticeship process. But many leaders may balk at the thought of "playing second fiddle" to any other person in the church – especially if the would-be apprentice has an impressive leadership resume. The value of the apprenticeship is manifold: it gives the newcomer a sense of the operating culture of the ministry, introduces him/her to the leadership style and quirks of the church, provides an opportunity to become more comfortable with the divisions of responsibility, and so forth.

One of the most beneficial products of the apprenticeship, though, is the demonstration of humility and servanthood signaled by one's willingness to work through the established process, regardless of personal experience or capacity. In one of the churches that we studied a 54-year old Senior Vice President of a Fortune 500 company joined the church and after a period of time was invited to participate as a leader. His first opportunity was to serve as an apprentice to a 31-year old auto mechanic who had served as a leader at the church for five years. When the accomplished businessman refused to do so, explaining that it was a waste of time and he had more experience and leadership wisdom than the younger, less educated man who would be his mentor, the church withdrew its offer to become involved as a leader. "It was quite tense," recalled the senior leader of the team to which the executive had been invited. "There is no doubt that John (the executive) had incredible experience and abilities. He had proven his skill level in the business world. In fact, his record of accomplishments was one of the things that caused us to want him to help us lead the church forward. He obviously had a lot of training and abilities that could help us.

"But our thought was that if John couldn't humble himself long enough to become a servant of someone who loves Christ and has a track record of good leadership in our church, then he wasn't spiritually mature enough to be a leader. We think of leadership as serving people, not ordering them around and producing results at any cost.

Our culture here is different than at (the executive's company), and I don't think John was ready to make that transition yet."

Inflexibility of Team Activity

Great teams must remain internally flexible. For instance, sometimes a Strategic Leader may have to temporarily provide operational leadership for the team while the Operational Leader is focused on an all-consuming effort that precludes his/her involvement in other aspects of the team's work at that time. Or the Team-Building Leader may have to serve as the Directing Leader while the latter is unavailable due to other commitments to the team. This is why it is so important for all of the team's members to learn from each other and to be constantly growing in their personal leadership capacity. Team theory permits us to cleanly differentiate and separate the responsibilities and activities of each team member; reality shows no respect for those divisions of labor. The more comfortable each team member becomes "covering" for a teammate, without trying to take over his/her area of emphasis, the more effective the team will become.

Harmful Expectations

Any time a major change is made within a ministry, people expect certain outcomes to result. Sometimes those outcomes are reasonable, but sometimes they are not. When expectations are out of line with reality, the change is doomed from the start. Yet, you do not want people's expectations to be so low that they lack excitement or enthusiasm related to the alteration being implemented. What are people's expectations of your solo leaders? How would those expectations change if you shift to lay teams providing direction to the ministry? How appropriate are those expectations?

Demanding Too Much, Too Soon

Switching from solo leadership to team-based leadership represents a huge transformation in church culture, ministry process, authority allocation, and people's thinking. A great transition process will get the congregation excited about the possibilities and have them anxiously anticipating the shift to a more effective, efficient and productive leadership paradigm. However, because people are uncomfortable with change and Americans are increasingly skeptical of the claims of superiority regarding new products, services or procedures, one of the pressures the transition team will face is that of producing results – quickly, broadly, perfectly and undeniably.

You may discover that the deeper the opposition to team-based leadership, the higher the initial expectations your opponents will set for the new approach. Instead of acknowledging and applauding improvements in practice and results, opponents will complain that the new approach has failed to produce perfection. Instead of appreciating the fact that more people are using their gifts and producing great ministry outcomes, detractors will focus on the fact that most people are not serving as leaders in the expanded leadership approach. Rather than celebrate greater efficiencies realized through leadership teams, resistance will be waged on the basis of the amount of time and energy that was devoted to the transition itself.

As you might imagine, conceding to the pressure to produce big results too quickly can completely destroy well-developed plans, growing momentum and small victories that eventually lead to significant gains. What can you do to protect the transition process and the potential of having a solid team-led ministry in anticipation of the demands that you produce big results quickly?

Six Steps Used To Great Affect By Other Churches

1. Before you initiate the process of change, gather your facts regarding the compelling reasons for the transition – including the harsh realities concerning the inefficiency and ineffectiveness of solo leadership at your church. Hopefully, these statistics, anecdotes and behavioral patterns will not have to be used in a confrontation regarding the need for the transition – but it will be helpful to have those facts readily available should they be needed.

2. From the start, monitor and modify people's expectations of what the transition will produce so that people's assumptions and hopes are reasonable. Examine how quickly they expect results, how much upheaval they anticipate as the church moves to a team-based culture, consider what they believe each leader will produce, and so forth. When their expectations are out of sync with reality, confront them and provide a more reasonable concept of likely results.

3. Do not launch into the process until you have consensus among all of the church's key leaders that team-based leadership is best for the church, and that the inevitable challenges and discomfort brought on by the transition will be compensated for by the enhanced ministry outcomes that result.

4. Begin the process with a pilot team whose experience will quietly and unobtrusively test the waters and help identify unexpected or unaddressed challenges regarding the process, the people or the productivity of the team approach within your church. By starting out small and outside of the scrutiny of the congregation you will increase the chance of scoring a big success when the process is expanded.

5. Once you have initiated the team process, do not hesitate to encourage congregants by pointing out the small, day to day victories achieved by your teams. People do not usually argue with successful outcomes. The more that they sense the team strategy is producing as desired, and that there is momentum building behind the team approach, the less likely they will be to mount an offensive against the new way of doing things.

6. Get everyone involved in the process. People feel a deeper sense of ownership when they are significantly involved in facilitating a meaningful ministry change. Those who own the process will be less prone to badmouthing it or refusing to acknowledge its value to the church. There are many possible avenues for assistance with the team transition, but one of the most powerful and useful is for non-leader congregants to pray for both the process and for the individuals involved in the process. Only a spiritually dysfunctional individual would pray for specific group and outcome, then work to undermine the prayed for outcomes through gossip, complaining, or political maneuvering.

Naturally, even if the transition produces results, there will be bumps and bruises along the way. Be ready to address the concerns of individuals whose support for teams was tenuous and will take advantage of the slightest opportunity to jump ship. These are not bad people, they are simply scared and lack a full understanding of the vision and value of teams. Help them stay focused, trusting and supportive.

A Dearth of Teams

In some small churches, pastors worry they do not have enough leaders to develop a wide range of teams. Sometimes the problem is not knowing what types of people to look for as leaders (i.e., searching for the superhero-as-leader types). In other situations the problem is not the absence of enough leaders but that the church is trying to do too much. Once the church develops a reasonable plan for growing its ministry capacity, then it can unleash teams on an as-needed or as-available basis.

Resist the temptation to assign any given team to "double duty" – i.e., taking on two or more dimensions of the ministry. As noted earlier, in relation to allowing individual leaders to serve on two or more teams, the energy, passion, vision and resources of the team become compromised, resulting in unsatisfying results.

Be Alert for Other Landmines!

Our research identified many other landmines that await churches moving into a team process. Hopefully, your sense of the philosophy behind the choices described above, as well as the concept of team-based lay leadership outlined in previous chapters, will prepare you to intelligently and strategically respond to the other challenges that will emerge as you pursue team leadership.

A SELF-
EXAMINATION

On occasion, life choices are either-or propositions: either you choose one option or you are left with the other. Americans dislike having such limited choices. We prefer the sense of control and power, as well as the pleasure of having truly disparate alternatives, derived from selecting from a broad range of possibilities. In the case of choosing your leadership approach – i.e., solo leadership or team leadership – it appears that you have an either-or challenge. Which option is best for you?

As you consider your answer,
keep the following observations in mind:

• Churches can only grow as much as their leaders will facilitate. The degree of growth made possible by teams of gifted leaders working together will generally exceed the growth feasible under a group of solo leaders.

• The more a church allows leaders to use their gifts and skills for ministry, the more leaders the church will attract and retain. The more leaders the church attracts and retains, the more likely the church is to develop a full-orbed, healthy ministry.

• It seems most likely that God's design for leadership is for individuals to work together in teams and thus minimize personal glory than for a single, solo leader to strive to make everything happen and receive the brunt of the church's attention. Team leadership permits the focus to remain on God; solo leadership deflects the spotlight from Him.

•   When personnel changes happen, the church is less likely to be crippled by the departure of one member from a team than to be crippled by the departure of the solo leader. The church will struggle in both situations, but the struggle will be less profound in the case of losing one team-based leader.

•   Quality in leadership is enhanced by constant and objective performance evaluation. Solo leaders have a relatively poor track record of self-evaluation when compared to the self-assessment of leadership teams.

•   In a solo leadership model, the qualification standards are high but the production standards are often unmet. In the team leadership model the qualification standards are not as lofty, but the productivity level is typically met or exceeded. The question for a church is whether it is more interested in impressing people with the quality of a small number of individuals or with the quality of what a larger number of team-based leaders produce.

Team-based leadership, utilizing the wealth of talents and abilities that God has invested in lay people, is not the answer to every challenge and dilemma facing the Church. The continued refusal to exploit those talents and abilities, however, leaves the Church at a disadvantage. The team approach may not solve every problem, but it often increases the potential for eliminating many of the vexing issues that perplex the Church.

Which Way Is Right For You?

To arrive at the best choice for your church, you might take an inventory of how your leadership process and output is presently faring. Answer these questions and reflect on whether team leadership or solo leadership is likely to facilitate improvements.

1. What is the vision for your church's ministry? How widely known and owned is that vision among your congregants?

2. What goals have you set in the past year in relation to your vision? How satisfactorily did your church meet all of those goals?

3. Is the Senior Pastor of your church a true leader? How well does he/she work with and develop other leaders? Would the pastor's productivity and personal well-being improve if your leadership model shifted?

4. What is your church's philosophy of leadership and leadership development? How confident are you that your philosophy is an ideal match with your congregation's needs?

5. How does your church identify potential lay leaders? How viable is that approach?

6. Once a lay leader is identified, what happens with them? What types of preparation and development do your lay leaders receive? How many of them voluntarily stay heavily involved as leaders for an extended period of service?

7. How do you ascertain the leadership aptitudes of your leaders? If you identify those distinctions, how do you apply that knowledge to the assignments given to your leaders?

8. Does your church culture foster team leadership or solo leadership? Is that intentional?

9. How many lay leaders have left your church because they felt that their gifts would never be adequately or appropriately used? How many left your church because they were burned out by your ministry?

10. How difficult is it to keep your lay leaders motivated to stay sharp and involved?

11. How does your church evaluate the effectiveness of its leaders? How effective is that evaluation process? How could it be improved?

12. Which approach would be of greatest benefit to your church: solo leadership or team leadership? If your church were to transition from one to the other, what price would be paid for that change?

Whether you determine that lay leadership teams or solo-based leadership is the best path for your church to pursue, my prayer is that you will empower every leader God has brought to your church to live up to his/her ministry and leadership potential. And all things being equal, I pray that your church will strongly consider the merits and benefits of employing lay leadership teams as your strategy for unleashing God's greatest blessings upon your ministry and those whom it will influence.

BIBLIOGRAPHY

Anderson, Leith. *Leadership That Works*. Minneapolis: Bethany House Publishers, 1999.

Barna, George. *Effective Lay Leadership Teams*. Ventura, CA: Issachar Resources, 2000.

———. *The Habits of Highly Effective Churches*. Ventura, CA: Regal Books, 2000.

———. *The Second Coming of the Church*. Nashville: Word Books, 1998.

———. (editor and contributor) *Leaders On Leadership*. Ventura, CA: Regal Books, 1997.

———. *Turning Vision Into Action*. Ventura, CA: Regal Books, 1996.

———. *Church Marketing: Breaking Ground for the Harvest*. Ventura, CA: Regal Books, 1992.

———. *The Power of Vision*. Ventura, CA: Regal Books, 1992.

Cordeiro, Wayne. *Doing Church as a Team*. Honolulu: New Hope Resources, 1998.

Cladis, George. *Leading the Team-Based Church*. San Francisco: Jossey-Bass Publishers, 1999.

Gangel, Kenneth. *Team Leadership in Christian Ministry*. Chicago: Moody Press, 1997.

Heenan, David and Warren Bennis. *Co-Leaders*. New York: John Wiley & Sons, 1999.

Katzenbach, Jon and Douglas Smith. *The Wisdom of Teams*. New York: Harper Business, 1993.

Katzenbach, Jon (editor). *The Work of Teams*. Boston: Harvard Business School Publishing, 1998.

Thrall, Bill, Bruce McNicol and Ken McElrath. *The Ascent of a Leader*. San Francisco: Jossey-Bass Publishers, 1999.

Wilkes, C. Gene. *Jesus On Leadership*. Wheaton, IL: Tyndale House Publishers, 1998.

ABOUT
GEORGE BARNA

George Barna is the president of the Barna Research Group, Ltd., a marketing research firm located in Ventura, CA. The company specializes in conducting primary research for Christian ministries and non-profit organizations. Since its inception in 1984, Barna Research has served several hundred parachurch ministries and numerous churches, in addition to various non-profit and for-profit organizations.

To date, Barna has written 29 books. His most recent works are *Rechurching the Unchurched*; *Growing True Disciples*; *Effective Lay Leadership Teams*; *Boiling Point*; and *The Habits of Highly Effective Churches*. Past works include best-sellers such as *The Frog in the Kettle*, *The Second Coming of the Church*, *User Friendly Churches*, *Marketing the Church* and *The Power of Vision*. Several of his books have received national awards. He has also written for numerous periodicals and has published more than two-dozen syndicated reports on a variety of topics related to ministry. His work is frequently cited as an authoritative source by the media.

Barna is also widely known for his intensive, research-based seminars for church leaders. He is a popular speaker at ministry conferences around the world, and has taught at several universities and seminaries. He has served as a pastor of a large, multi-ethnic church and has served on several boards of directors. He is the founding director of The Barna Institute, a non-profit organization dedicated to providing strategic information to ministries.

After graduating summa cum laude in Sociology from Boston College, Barna earned two Masters degrees from Rutgers University. He also received a doctorate from Dallas Baptist University.

He lives with his wife Nancy and their two daughters (Samantha and Corban) in southern California. He enjoys spending time with his family, writing, reading, playing basketball and guitar, relaxing on the beach and visiting bookstores.

About the Barna Research Group, Ltd.

The Barna Research Group, Ltd. (BRG) is a full-service marketing research company located in Ventura, California. BRG has been providing information and analysis regarding cultural trends, ministry practices, marketing and business strategy, fundraising, worldviews and leadership since 1984. The vision of the company is to provide Christian ministries with current, accurate, and reliable information in bite-sized pieces and at affordable prices, to facilitate effective and strategic decision-making.

BRG conducts both quantitative and qualitative research using a variety of data collection methods, with particular emphasis upon the application of the results. The company conducts more research within the Christian community than any other organization in the U.S. and regularly releases reports describing its findings regarding the values, attitudes, lifestyles, religious beliefs and religious practices of adults and teenagers, as well as the current state of churches. That information is also accessible through the seminars, books, website and tapes produced by BRG.

To access many of the findings of BRG, visit the company's web site at www.barna.org. You will have access to the free bi-monthly reports (*The Barna Update*) published on the site; a data archives that provides current statistics in relation to forty aspects of ministry and lifestyle; the various resources produced by George Barna and the Barna Research Group; and information about upcoming seminars as well as the firm's research activities. If you wish to receive *The Barna Update* by e-mail every two weeks, you may sign up for that free service on the home page of the site.

To contact the Barna Research Group, call 805-658-8885 or write to 5528 Everglades Street, Ventura, CA 93003.